CUT LOOSE YOUR
STAMMERING TONGUE

CUT LOOSE YOUR STAMMERING TONGUE

Black Theology in the Slave Narratives

Edited by
Dwight N. Hopkins
and
George C. L. Cummings

ORBIS BOOKS

Maryknoll, New York 10545

Second Printing, July 1992

The Catholic Foreign Mission Society of America (Maryknoll) recruits and trains people for overseas missionary service. Through Orbis Books, Maryknoll aims to foster the international dialogue that is essential to mission. The books published, however, reflect the opinions of their authors and are not meant to represent the official position of the society.

Library of Congress Cataloging-in-Publication Data

Cut loose your stammering tongue : black theology in the slave
  narratives / edited by Dwight N. Hopkins and George C. L. Cummings.
        p.   cm.
    Includes index.
    ISBN 0-88344-774-6
    1. Black theology—History.   2. Slaves' writings. American—
History and criticism.   3. Slaves—United States—Religious life.
4. Afro-Americans—Religion.   I. Hopkins, Dwight N.   II. Cummings,
George C. L.
BT82.7.C87   1991
230'.089'96073—dc20   91-27967
                                                            CIP

"Go in peace, fearing no man, for lo! I have cut loose your stammering tongue and unstopped your deaf ears. A witness shalt thou be, and thou shalt speak to multitudes, and they shall hear. My word has gone forth, and it is power. Be strong and lo! I am with you even until the world shall end. Amen."

(From an anonymous slave narrative)

CONTENTS

Introduction

DWIGHT N. HOPKINS

Oh Freedom! Oh Freedom!
Oh Freedom Over Me!
And 'fore I Be a Slave,
I Be Buried in My Grave,
And Go Home to My Lord
And Be Free!
(Slave spiritual)

In 1865 the Civil War concluded. As a byproduct of this vio-
lent conflict between North and South, four million African
Americans tasted freedom for the first time since they were
initially dragged from their original homeland on the shores of
the African continent. From that time in 1619 until the end of
the Civil War, enslaved Africans had molded themselves into
something new — an African American people. The slaves were
not simply idle victims of brute white force. On the contrary,
they created a world around them that was sometimes visible,
but incomprehensible, to the slave master. Their dogged and
creative strength fashioned a new black collective self behind
the closed doors in the slave quarters or deep in the woods late
at night. Here slaves developed a culture of survival that
included all the dimensions of a thriving but enchained community. Politicians and orators emerged to figure out how to
deal with the daily unequal power relations with white folks.
Musicians and dancers came forth to bring joy and relaxation
to a people burdened with slavery. Cooks baked a mixture of
African foods with white European delicacies and helped their

ix

community survive the meager rations allotted by the Big House. Economists made sure the slave owners felt satisfied with the daily output of their human property and, at the same time, devised a "new" mathematics that gave bondswomen and bondsmen material benefits without the masters' detecting any of their losses. Storytellers sat around and related tales from Africa, weaving a thread of history, folklore, survival, and freedom that educated each generation in African American traditions. In all this diverse formation and re-formation of a collective African American being, a new people in the hell of slavery, the most common bond among all who suffered as chattel was slave religion.

Slaves sang songs to heaven during backbreaking work in the cotton and sugarcane fields, or even as they drove "Massa" in his buggy from plantation to plantation. Work chain-gangs of young virile adult males could be heard far and wide singing religious tunes in an African call-and-response style. Cooks hummed praise moans to Jesus as they prepared supper for the Big House. Black nannies cooed well-known spirituals to white babies suckling black nipples. Religious expressions respected no boundaries between appointed hours of worship and so-called secular time. But the most concentrated worship space was found in the "Invisible Institution"[1] — the illegal and concealed slave gatherings where full singing, dancing, preaching, praying, and shouting were offered as testimonies to what the Lord had done for black people in bondage.

Out of this richly layered new reality called the African American community, crafted by the slaves themselves, we find a fresh way of understanding the relation between an oppressed people's belief in God and God's covenant of grace and freedom for God's faithful. In narratives recorded during the 1930s the profound belief in a God present with them through trials and tribulations, the One who would bring them to freedom, rings clear. These stories of former slaves open up a new world of faith and life and thereby unveil a unique divine presence with the poor.

THE NARRATIVES AS SOURCES

The contributors to *Cut Loose Your Stammering Tongue* bring together research from the spirituals, slave autobiographies, and the narratives. But this book relies mainly on forty-one volumes of interviews with former slaves recorded in George P. Rawick's *The American Slave: A Composite Autobiography*.[2] Known as the Slave Narrative Collection, these volumes resulted from the 1936-38 work of the Folklore Division of the Federal Writers' Project. The Federal Works Administration (under Franklin D. Roosevelt's presidency) established the Project as one means of white-collar employment during the depression years. The Slave Narrative Collection comprises roughly twenty thousand pages of interviews with ex-slaves. There are also several states' Writers Projects that did not reach the federal office. The Virginia Writers' Project was published as *Weevils in the Wheat: Interviews with Virginia Ex-Slaves*; Georgia's in *Drums and Shadows: Survival Studies Among the Georgia Coastal Negroes*; and Louisiana's in *Gumbo Ya-Ya: Folk Tales of Louisiana*. The American Freedmen's Inquiry Commission of 1863 also conducted forty-eight interviews. Finally, over four hundred (non–Slave Narrative Collection) Louisiana interviews are found in the Southern University archives in Louisiana.[3]

However, the Slave Narrative Collection languished for quite some time in the dusty rooms of the Library of Congress. Ulrich B. Phillips, a Georgia-born Yale professor, had posed profound questions regarding the narratives' authenticity. This was not a light matter. Phillips, considered the "historian's historian," dismissed the words of the former slaves with this claim: "Ex-slave narratives in general were issued with so much abolitionist editing that as a class, their authenticity is doubtful." This statement epitomized the rest of Phillips's 1929 *Life and Labor in the Old South*.[4] Unfortunately, it took forty years before scholarship began to refute the extremely biased, if not racist, research by Phillips. The year 1972 marked a qualitative turning point for slave narrative scholarship. At that time Eugene D. Genovese's *Roll, Jordan, Roll: The World the Slaves Made* came off the presses. Perhaps even more significant were the publications that year by two African American scholars: volume one of *The American Slave: A Composite Autobiography*, edited by George P. Rawick (discussed above); and *The Slave Community: Plantation Life in the Antebellum South*, by John W. Blassingame.[5] Rawick began to make the Slave Narrative Collection available to the public for the first time, and Blassingame's text pioneered research into establishing the contours of the slave community from the words and thoughts of the slaves themselves.[6]

Despite these and other sound refutations of the pro-white-supremacist arguments of Phillips, some questions do linger in terms of the Slave Narrative Collection's legitimacy and reliability. For instance, the majority of the interviewers were white, and this could have dampened the full force and truth of poor blacks' speech; the narratives involving black interviewers elicit a more straightforward response on the part of former slaves. Two comments are in order here. In order to assess the responses reported by white interviewers, one can, first of all, corroborate these results by contrasting them with those of black interviewers. Specifically, the Virginia Writers' Project (*Weevils in the Wheat*) was a product of twenty interviewers, thirteen of whom were African American. The Louisiana Writers' Project (*Gumbo Ya-Ya*) involved many black questioners. Blacks made up eight of the eleven interviewers in Florida. And volumes 18 and 19 of Rawick's work were carried out by an all-black group of cultural workers from Fisk University. Second, that ex-slaves dared to risk self-exposure in order to share so much with white interviewers about the horror of slavery and the blacks' thirst for freedom is a tribute to the courage of the interviewees and, in many cases, a demonstration of their reluctance to conceal the most fiendish examples of the antebellum South.

To a certain degree we also have to allow for suspicion about the narratives based on the ages of these black informants. They were all roughly seventy years removed from slavery when interviewed. About one-third were less than 5 years old when the Civil War ended in 1865; another third were born before 1851. This "too old" argument falls because there is no *necessary* correlation between aging and memory loss. Perhaps the elderly have more time and thus spend more time reviewing the details of their lives.

Finally, we can group together possible complaints that the Slave Narrative Collection has too many internal contradictions, that the slaves were illiterate, or that they recounted tales of fiction as fact. Any objective scholar would have to agree that all source documents for historical reconstruction contain degrees of internal contradiction. If we demanded absolute consistency, we would be forced to question the authenticity of most North American history, which has been written by and from the perspective of privileged white males. Instead, we should employ the same research principles one uses in all historiography—compare and cross reference slave narratives with other historical documentation.[7] Scores of antebellum and postbellum ex-slave autobiographies abound. Slave testimonies, moreover, appear in diaries; folklore; speeches; sermons; letters; pre–Civil War publications; church, legislative, and judicial records; petitions; abolitionist newspapers; major newspapers during that time, such as the *New York Times*; scholarly journals; private printings; and broadsides, just to name a few primary source-corroborating witnesses. Thus the Slave Narrative Collection is one part of a more than two-century-long genre. As Marion Wilson Starling concludes:

> The autobiographical record of George Washington Carver, published in 1944, is the last of more than six thousand extant narratives of American Negro slaves, the first of which was published nearly two and a half centuries ago, the narrative of one Adam, "servant of John Saffin, Esquire," printed in Boston in 1703.[8]

Contributions to Religious Scholarship

Building on a contemporary black theological movement, *Cut Loose Your Stammering Tongue* falls within a quarter-of-a-century tradition of African American scholarship elaborating black Americans' experience with God. Its strength lies in literally developing *black theology* from the actual voices of poor, enslaved African Americans.[9] To appreciate this contribution, a brief look at contemporary black theological developments is helpful.[10]

Contemporary black theology began with the formation of the ad hoc National Committee of Negro Churchmen in the summer of 1966, specifically with the publication of their "Black Power Statement" in the *New York Times* (31 July 1966). This stage witnessed primarily radical black clergy, who debated theological issues with their white counterparts and charted aspects of a beginning black theology. They claimed that black power and black consciousness revealed the presence of Jesus Christ the Liberator. Furthermore, they asserted that the essence of Christianity was deliverance of and freedom for the oppressed on earth.[11]

The Society for the Study of Black Religion (1970) marked black theology's transformation into stage two, an academic discipline in which black religious scholars emphasized religious issues among themselves. Here black theologians struggled over the relation between liberation and reconciliation, God's goodness and human suffering, African religion and black theology, and the spontaneous faith expressions of black people versus the theological systems of the white academy.

Stage three, in the mid-1970s, gave birth to the Black Theology Project comprised of church persons, community activists, and scholars, with a strong connection between African Americans and the Third World. The broad range of participants reflected black theology's turn toward liberation theologies in the Third World, the day-to-day survival issues in the black community, black theology's relation to the black church, and the importance of feminism and Marxist analysis.

The fourth and present stage commenced around the mid-1980s. Its characteristics are the growth of younger African American thinkers, who emphasize an exploration of theology from any and all aspects of black life, and most strikingly, the cutting edge challenge of womanists (black female religious scholars), who have pressed for a holistic black theology that entails an integration of race, class, gender, and sexual orientation analyses. Womanists have shown the urgency of doing black theology from such innovative sources as black fiction and women's roles in the Bible.

Cut Loose Your Stammering Tongue is deeply indebted to this tradition. But what it hopes to develop further is a method of African American theology and black religion where the *main* resource for black action and talk about God arises out of the lives and words of *poor* black people's faith. We hold that the original premises of black theology, signified most clearly by James H. Cone (emphasizing Christian liberation) and Gayraud S. Wilmore (stressing non-Christian liberation), still remain true. The question is how to develop further that foundational framework—the unity and distinction between Christian and non-Christian, church and non-church, and theological and religious resources in African American faith and life.

At least one important task, we believe, for today's black theology is learning from the liberating faith that comes out of the actual mouths of the poor. What does it mean for a black theology of liberation if the main authorities for theology are Euro-Americans? How can we move beyond a mode of research and writing that footnotes preponderantly African Americans who talk about the black oppressed but who themselves are highly educated and middle class? The issue here is not a debate about the elite education and middle-class status of black theologians. We concur on the important role of African American "cultural workers" or "organic intellectuals" or "grounded theologians" in the struggle for black liberation and full humanity. The issue is whether we will use our highly privileged positions—which arose from the sacrifice of poor people—to mediate and privilege poor people's silenced voices. Of course, a certain degree of filtering will take place, with our voices leveraging the words of those from the underside of history. And, of course, we risk the actual obscuring of a poor African American perspective. But we want to press ourselves and those concerned with faith and life to find new ways radically to put the black poor—the primary voice—at the center of African American religious scholarship. Perhaps the most promising indications in this direction are black female religious writers.[12] Basically, we need to be accountable to those less privileged in our communities who have neither the time nor the resources to say a word about their faith in a God who has made a way out of no way in their trials and tribulations.

THE SLAVE NARRATIVE IN DIALOGUE

The narratives of slaves and ex-slaves in the USA provide foundational elements for the creation of a constructive black theology of liberation. The religious voices and thoughts of African American chattel do not, however, operate in a passive, non-initiating manner. As a living source and a medium of God's word in action, they compel black theology to deepen further its reliance on indigenous resources in the African American church and community, thereby commanding black theology to cut loose its stammering tongue. Seen negatively, primary interpretation from language, thought forms, and practices alien and harmful to an African American theological discussion will ensure a stuttering in black talk about and experience with God. Put positively, the slaves' faithful story about freedom helps to unleash the full power of African American speech, which reflects and plumbs the depths of God's grace of freedom to the black poor. Slaves don't stammer; they speak God's truth.

Furthermore, the slave narratives tell black theology to cut loose its stammering tongue with at least four "words" of ancestral wisdom. First, they tell us to hear and heed the life-language of our chained forebears. Centuries of distance between the first enslaved Africans brought to the so-called New World by white European Christians have tended to shadow the ever present cloud of witnesses around the black poor. Our religious ancestors have never left us, and they have never ceased talking to us. However, black theology has to persist in opening its ears and its mind within the very historical theological amnesia forced upon it by white Christian supremacist practices in church, academy, and the broader society.

Second, black slaves remove obstacles from our "God-talk" by imbuing us with their unique liberation practice, world-view, language, thought patterns, and theological common sense. In contrast, years of white education, particularly white theological training, have infused an alien and unnatural method of thinking into the subconscious of African American religious thought. Consequently, we who attempt to talk about the liberating faith of oppressed black folk and allow that same empowering belief and spirituality to talk through us must return to our theological beginnings. In a sense, the slaves' religious stories are a calling for us to write our way back home.

Third, slaves' language, thought, and practice show us how God presents God's particular self in the constrained, marred lives of a faith-freed, beautiful, black people. In other words, our search for seeds and resources in the slave story tells us that God dwells among the most unimportant and despised "citizens" in the USA. This proves that good news still lives. Given an increasing drive toward instantaneous consumer gratification, latent itching for war, personal insecurity, and pyramidal wealth stratification in religious educational schools, churches, and the broader society, the poor *need* to hear unfettered good news. They need to know about unstammering straight talk from the Lord.

Fourth, the volumes of slave narratives provide a theological abundance of religious experience from non-Christian bearers of God's freeing spirit. In this way our enslaved ancestors attempt to cut loose our stammering tongue by sweeping aside any debilitating Christocentrism. In fact, God often infused the liberating Spirit in both Christian and non-Christian bondsmen and bondswomen as they lived and died for freedom. The Christian role in a black theology of liberation can draw renewed strength from knowing that God's freeing power blows wherever and however God wishes to blow. Like a black jazz quartet, slave stories may at first appear at odds, with both Christian and con-juring "instruments" all wailing at the same time. But after more profound listening, we discover that in many places the bass beat of liberation brings them all together.

The slaves' faith in freedom never died, even in the face of an apparent everlasting evil. The slaves maintained their human-ity with a steadfast hope in liberation as their ultimate concern. Some African American chattel fought individually. Others organized collectively. Some simply packed up and ran north to "Canaan." Still others gave up any ideas of achieving heaven on earth in their lifetime and waited for death to transport them across Jordan to see their Maker. Moreover, apparently some slaves felt that their individual slave plantations were much bet-ter than their neighbors'. But rarely, if at all, do we discover any enslaved African American equating, and thereby justifying, the demonic nature of slavery with the Bible or God's will and pur-pose for humanity. And it is in black chattel's faith in God's free intent for humanity that a universal note sounds in our ears. Despite what the slavery world said, God had a plan for all human beings, black and white, slave and free to share the earth equally in freedom.

With these "words" above, and others, the slave narratives,

as God's medium, are telling black theology, "Cut loose your stammering tongue."

To our theological sisters and brothers doing theology in the Third World, we offer our work as an act of solidarity. The writing of liberation theologies is flourishing throughout Africa, Asia, Latin America, and the USA; it is the freshest breath of the Divine working in the religious and theological field today. Religious academicians, pastors, and lay persons from Africa, Asia, and Latin America, as well as people of color and women in the USA, have been in the forefront of these developments.[13] It is important for people victimized by the same false interpretation of Christianity and the same religious, political, cultural, and economic systems linked to that interpretation, to extend hands in complementary projects. The slave narratives exemplify, we contend, one voice of the voiceless in the third-world theological movement. It offers liberation theologies the complexity and interrelatedness of indigenous culture, politics, economics, language, thought forms, and metaphors born out of the mouths of the very people we seek to be with, speak with, and write with.

The narratives, moreover, encourage us to continue to liberate liberation theologies by avoiding the harmful methodologies of dominating theologies, which periodically claim something theologically new or relevant while, in actuality, preserving the status quo of personal and systemic privileges within the monastery-like hideouts of the academy. To dare to speak with and for those without means to speak, then, implies liberation theologians checking ourselves by allowing the poor to critique us and also lovingly critiquing the poor. The test of liberation is not its newness or our assertions about liberation. Rather, our proximity to God's involvement with society's marginalized and that movement's conversion of us set our agenda and its authenticity.

Similarly, the narratives interrogate our commitment to the Christian church (and other forms of liberation faith communities). Slaves met God in "bush arbor" congregations of the "Invisible Institution." They had to meet secretly in order to worship a God who related divine compassion to the crucible of suffering of poor folk in pain. If they could risk their lives to hear the word of the Lord in communal settings, we too must forever be clear that theology bubbles up from our respective church communities. And to accept the calling of theologians, we are forever bound to the spiritual ties of our faith contexts.

Does liberation theology generate from the heads of liberation theologians? The testimonies of African American slaves answer in the negative. From these faith perspectives, any "doing" of theology without a communal faith connection is simply sitting on the front porch of the slave master's white house with our legs crossed, sipping mint juleps with our oppressors. At one point or another we all taste the sugar-coated seduction of the dominating white theological talk in the "white house." The white-controlled academy and church administration settings can create a mirage where we think that place is the actual basis for doing theology. Though academic space can facilitate theological work, such a state as our primary existence can pump us up, especially when we lift up the agendas of the academy or white-church hierarchy. Yet any knowledge of poor and marginalized folk worship, particularly revealed by God's presence in slave stories, jolts us again into realizing that dominating theologies are foreign elements and, in most cases, intent on maintaining the status of slavery for the enslaved. Accordingly, to hear poor people praise God and listen to their testimonies of how that divine encounter frees them to survive and struggle day by day is basic to the further liberation of liberation theology. A struggling people of faith is the community for liberation theology.

Furthermore, the tongues of ex-slaves do not say which of their pains is more important than other kinds of suffering; nor do they fixate on which path to the kingdom is central to the liberation movement. These enslaved simple folk show a sophisticated concern to reach their cultural humanity *along with* a simultaneous struggle against systemic political-economic evils. Likewise, they understand class analysis while also using their own African American religious language to fight against "normative" European and Euro-American speech. Slave religious faith did not hold one form of struggle (whether religious, cultural, political, economic, or linguistic) above all others; God's spirit for them was a holistic movement calling forth an integrated, coordinated struggle for human life. The multidimensional faith expressions of the poor continue to be both a stumbling block and challenge to liberation theologians.

Finally, we offer this book as an effective model for theological scholarship. The authors of the first three chapters have met together regularly for the last two and a half years. In that period the Spirit and our ancestors' spirits have revealed the liberating power of sharing together the potency of non-hierarchical research and writing. Our group, the BT Forum,[14] has been a work space for encouraging vision, intellectual struggle, criticism, and self-criticism. We have witnessed the importance of maintaining a black theological place as one small act of doing liberation theology in "hand-to-hand combat" in the academy. Yet this model has sustained more than our theological hopes and imagination. We've also shared our personal growth. Specifically, we have attempted to persist in reviewing this question: What does it mean for an individual to be called by God to be an African American theologian for the church and society? That question continues to haunt us because of the magnitude of its implications. What we are discovering is how God's Spirit brings a renewed grace of empowering faith by calling the theologian over and over again to the task. At certain points clarity about the task breaks through. However, the dynamic of growing into a prophetic theologian remains forever somewhat elusive. Yet, because this calling is one toward community, energy comes to the individual in the communal effort. The individual theologian's internal faith in God's will couples with his or her connection to a community of faith. This system of overlapping checks and balances (individual and collective interpretations of God's plan) facilitates growing into the role of theologian.

Our nearly three years of birthing has shown us that black theological liberation work can seem overwhelming. But the real joy is in service to our people wherever they may be—church, community, or academy. *Cut Loose Your Stammering Tongue* is one of the service projects that the BT Forum has attempted. We have also spoken on panels in the academy, done radio and cable television shows, preached about the slave narratives from church pulpits (two of us are ordained Baptists and one is Presbyterian), and held theological retreats. Feeling a sense of calling to the church community, we've tried to foster the continuance of black theology by providing avenues for first- and second-generation black religious scholars to dialogue about the future. Each generation, we believe, builds on and is indebted to the preceding one; the future springs out of the past and present. Ultimately, the cutting loose of stammering tongues is a communal liberation undertaking.

UNITY AND DIVERSITY

To help black religious scholarship further turn the corner to society's African American marginalized, the contributors to this book seek to answer one unified question: How can we draw out from slave religion some liberating theological and ethical practices for a black theology of liberation today? We explore new theological and religious categories that the slaves present to us on their own terms. At some points we engage traditional doctrines arising out of the black church, verifying some and infusing others with new substance. White theological constructs, in some instances, are used in order to shed new light on slave religious experience. At times the language, humor, and thought forms of the slaves refuse categorization or correlation with anything we have previously encountered; in such cases they simply force us to present them as they are. The reader will also note that the "tongues" of the contributors still "stammer." This is not a comment on the slave narratives, but more a statement about the extent of conversion we need to undergo before we approach the liberating faith of our ancestors. We all are struggling to "write our way back home," but the struggle is a difficult and protracted one.

In Chapter 1 Dwight N. Hopkins argues that African American slaves developed a unique and coherent understanding of Christianity based on creatively combining a way of life from their previous African sacred beliefs with the Christianity introduced to them by white North American missionaries. This African-Christian mixture produced a vibrant and emancipating slave Christian theology.

Hopkins's chapter traces the slaves' theological encounters with God, Jesus Christ, and human action. In each of these experiences, slaves' theological thought seems to have centered on at least three religious concerns — politics, culture, and a compassion for the poor. For example, African American bondservants pictured God with a political dimension. They saw a direct life-and-death power struggle between serving their God and serving the white slave masters' god. In the midst of this fight, slave religious belief maintained cultural expressions original to its African traditions and later to African American customs; slaves chose to worship God in their own language and dialect. They used one speech for the master and another among themselves. This dynamic interplay between culture and politics was grounded in God's freedom for the poor.

While agreeing with Hopkins on the liberating power of slave church teachings, George C. L. Cummings in Chapter 2 looks at the Christian Spirit and the coming of the Kingdom in slave interviews. He states that black theology needs to incorporate into its practice the perspectives that convey the fundamental hopes of black oppressed people. This statement, Cummings believes, reflects the need to deepen the "thematic universe" of the black poor. Therefore his chapter examines the slave narratives as a type of religious literature coming from the bottom of the African American community. To accomplish this task, Cummings includes an exploration of the world-view of the slaves as it affected their religious experience, and an interpretation of the theological expressions of the slaves in reference to the Spirit and eschatology.

Unlike Hopkins and Cummings, Will Coleman focuses in Chapter 3 more on how slave stories use religious language for their liberation struggle. Toward this end Coleman investigates different types of spirits to discover the ways in which slaves understood their relationship to the spiritual realm of their gods, goddesses, ancestors and ancestresses. He is especially interested in the borderline or transitional phase between a traditional African experience of the spiritual world (through dreams, visions, and possession) within the North American context, and a more thoroughly Christian one. The roles of the priest, priestess, conjurer, and early African American preacher or prophetess as a mediator of the sacred are also taken into account.

With Cheryl J. Sanders, in Chapter 4, we move from theology

to ethics. She turns our attention from a liberation theology and language in black theology to the development of a liberation ethic. Sanders targets a set group of slave conversion stories to show the diversity of slave moral and ethical options. If religious conversion caused a significant reorientation of bondservants in moral terms, she states, how did conversion affect the converts' attitudes toward slavery? Basically her research finds that the slave convert either condemns slavery or offers no self-conscious evaluation of slavery; not one person defends slavery on the basis of Christian ethics.

The concluding chapter of this text draws together some of the major lessons that the authors suggest and charts a basic outline for a constructive black theology of liberation today.

In *Cut Loose Your Stammering Tongue*, therefore, the contributors undertake the risk of mining the fresh, illiterate voices of those poor African American ex-slaves who have been silenced by the dominant theological scholarship and, unfortunately, missed in most black religious intellectual work. Admittedly, we risk skewing the very task we have set out to accomplish. Still, we wish to be converted by the sacred world-views, language, metaphors, and practices of former slaves in order to be more faithful to our own African American theological traditions in which faith, thought, and witness converge in God's movement toward a more free humanity—a radical freeing of the individual and society. If our work helps to loose the stammering tongues of all people who believe in the divine intent for a full humanity, then it will have advanced the mission of a black theology of liberation.

My word has gone forth, and it is power. Be strong and lo! I am with you even until the world shall end. Amen.[15]

1

SLAVE THEOLOGY
IN THE "INVISIBLE INSTITUTION"

DWIGHT N. HOPKINS

*My uncle, Ben, he could read de Bible, and he allus tell us
some day us be free. And Massa Henry laugh, "Haw, haw,
haw." And he say, "Hell, no, yous never be free. Yous ain't
got sense 'nuf to make de livin', if yous was free." Den, he
takes de Bible 'way from Uncle Ben and say it put de bad
ideas in he head, but Uncle gits 'nother Bible and hides it,
and Massa never finds out.*

(John Bates, ex-slave)

The black church begins in slavery; thus slave religion provides the first source for a contemporary statement on black
theology. The black church's unique tradition springs from the
emerging theology of African American chattel. While white
masters attempted to force their Christianity onto their black
property, slaves worshiped God secretly. Out of these illegal and
hidden religious practices, the "Invisible Institution," black
Christianity and black theology arose. Though chained and illiterate, black people dared to *think* theologically by testifying to
what the God of Moses had done for them. For example, recording the Christian substance of the spirituals—the novel religious

songs created by blacks under slavery—Colonel Thomas Wentworth Higginson, a white officer in the Civil War, observed:

> [The slaves'] memories are a vast bewildered chaos of Jew-
> ish history and biography; and most of the great events of
> the past, down to the period of the American Revolution,
> they instinctively attribute to Moses.[1]

Unfortunately, Higginson described these penetrating theological insights of the unlettered black bondservants as "bewildered chaos." He failed to appreciate the hermeneutical insights
of the poor. For the slaves, Moses acted as a human instrument
of divine liberation, because Yahweh had utilized him to eman-
cipate the slaves. If Yahweh could do this against Pharaoh, then
surely Yahweh had brought about all "the great events" of liberation movements, including the American Revolution against
the British oppressors. Furthermore, because the black slaves
identified themselves with the biblical Hebrew slaves and
because Yahweh had continued to act in human history, black
American bondsmen and bondswomen maintained hope and
certainty for their own deliverance from the cauldron of white
American chattel. Consequently this "bewildered chaos," in
fact, marked the slaves' developing theological critique from the
Bible's powerless voices.

An examination of slaves' lives and thought about God con-
veys several important factors in the religious lineage of the
black church. For instance, slave theology consistently experienced God dwelling with those in bondage, personal and systemic. The black religious experience prevented any separation
between the sacred and the secular, the church and the community. On the contrary, in the "Invisible Institution" black theology grew out of the community and the "church." As a result,
God ruled with unquestioned omnipotence and realized release
from total captivity. And *Jesus* assumed an intimate and kingly
relationship with the poor black chattel. Slaves emphasized both
the suffering human Jesus as well as Jesus' warrior ability to set
the downtrodden free. Moreover, the slaves distinguished their
humanity from the white slave master. For blacks, God and Jesus

called them to use all means possible to pursue religiously a human status of equality.

Furthermore, in radical distinction to white Christianity, religious encounters in ex-slave narratives, autobiographies, and the spirituals suggest an alternative theological interpretation with at least two aspects. First, African American slaves pictured a political dimension in their theology. They saw a direct political power struggle between serving their God and serving the white slave master's god. In certain situations whites claimed to be God on earth and mandated black submissiveness to a white idolatry that contradicted the slaves' loyalty to God's ultimacy.

Second, slaves' religious thought accented an original cultural expression. Not only did the slaves wage a political battle for the supremacy of their liberator God, but they also chose to worship this God in their own language and idiom, and in the extraordinary clandestineness of their own black religious community. Thus God's self was manifested in the specific textures of an African American slave story.

Today's black theology, church, and community need to be thankful that God spared a few formerly enslaved African Americans to pass on this black theological tradition. In the words of an ex-slave, John Brown, who gave praises to God for the opportunity to tell it like it actually was, we read:

> Lord! have mercy! have um mercy! Lord you done spared
> a few un us to tell de tale um, um, um, bout how hit was
> um, um wid us poor folks in dem days um, um, um. We
> done pray for dis day to come of freedom.[2]

Before we look at specific examples of how slaves told their story about the coming of freedom (through the slaves' black theology expressed in their experiences with God, Jesus, and human purpose), we investigate and define the contours of the "Invisible Institution" — the religious organization that served as the backdrop for the slaves' black theology.

THE CONTOURS OF THE "INVISIBLE INSTITUTION"

FROM THE SLAVES' PERSPECTIVE

To tell the slaves' religious story as the first source for today's black theology, one has to acknowledge the convergence of a reinterpreted white Christianity with the remains of African religions under slavery. It was precisely in the "Invisible Institution" that slaves synthesized these two foundational God-encounters to form slave theology.

Though slaves did not have direct access to the specifics of their former African religious practices and beliefs, they did maintain some theological remains — religious Africanisms. Unfortunately, the European slave trade, the practice of mixing Africans from different villages, the prohibition by white people of the use of African languages, and the fading memories of succeeding slave progeny[3] all served to dampen the vibrancy of a coherent African theology in slave thought. Nevertheless, enslaved Africans brought religious ideas and forces of theological habit with them to the "New World."

These Africans in bondage were not ignorant theologically. On the contrary, it was their structural religious world-view of God, Jesus, and human action that sustained them against the racist assaults of European slavers and their descendants in the "New World." Yet despite the existence of the slaves' black theology, white people continued to brand enslaved Africans as biologically subhuman, culturally uncivilized, and religiously heathen. Note the following emphasis of a prominent white missionary to Africa:

> I arrived at Bende to attempt anew the dredging and purifying of that ugly jungle pool of heathenism, with its ooze-life of shocking cruelty, reptilian passions and sprouting evil, spreading itself broad in the shadows amidst the most fruitful land on earth. ... Thus Christianity views her domain-to-be, lifting herself high above the secret springs of paganism's turgid streams below.[4]

Here whites endow Africans with reptilian qualities of passion and an inherent theological anthropology of evil. Conversely, white theology and white Christianity were normative and by definition superior ("lifting herself high above"), hence by nature dominating ("Christianity views her domain-to-be"). For white missionaries, who accompanied European slave traders to Africa, African communities offered no points of convergence for Christianity and African traditional religions. Instead of seeking points of theological contact with African indigenous religions, white theology served as the religious justification for Christian colonialism and racist plundering of black lands ("the most fruitful land on earth").

But Africans, even as they were bound as booty for the "New World," survived and resisted by remembering and relying on their traditional religions. And it is this primordial religious reflex that was bequeathed to the future black slaves in the "Invisible Institution."

THE AFRICAN CONTRIBUTION TO SLAVE THEOLOGY

Enslaved Africans brought a distinct perception of God to North America. African traditional religions described their ultimate divinity as the High God. "God has nowhere or nowhen" speaks to the omnipresence and non-derivative status of the divinity.[5] Some even called God "the Almighty," denoting divine omnipotence. By unbounded power God can do all things in heaven and on earth. This power is also what enables human beings to achieve their goals. God is both transcendent and immanent in African traditional religions. And God's authority entails all of creation. As the first and last cause, God created all things and thus holds the ultimate and final power over the visible and invisible creations. Humanity is contingent, but God is absolute authority.[6]

Furthermore, African indigenous religions believe in a God who cares; some call God "the Compassionate One," others see "the God of pity," who rescues victims in need. God is kind and "looks after the case of the poor man." In fact, God is the main hope of the poor in society. As Guardian and Keeper, God is named "the Protector of the poor" by some African traditional religions. They further specify that "there is a Saviour and only he can keep our lives."[7] As judge, God metes out justice, punishment, and retribution. Similarly, God displays protectiveness by avenging injustice. God is a divinity of partiality to the victim; God sides with the political powerlessness of society's injured.

In addition to these definite attributes of God, the theological framework shared by enslaved Africans in the "New World" also included a belief in theological anthropology—what it means to be God's created humanity.

African traditional religions shared a belief in a dynamic and interdependent relation between the individual and the community. The latter defined the former. Individualism proved anathema. To be human meant to stand in connection with the larger community of invisible ancestors and God and, of course, the visible community and family.

Africans recognize life as life-in-community. We can

> truly know ourselves if we remain true to our community, past and present. The concept of individual success or failure is secondary. . . . Our nature as beings-in-relation is a two-way relation: with God and with our fellow human-beings.[8]

African religions gave rise to a dynamic interplay between community and individual. Whatever happened to the communal gathering affected the individual, and whatever happened to the individual had an impact on the community. Such a theological view of humanity cuts across bourgeois notions of white Christianity's individualism and "me-first-ism." It seeks to forge a group solidarity and identity, beginning with God, proceeding through the ancestors to the community and immediate family, and continuing even to the unborn. One cannot be a human being unless one becomes a part of, feels a responsibility to, and serves the community. To preserve the community's well-being (through liberation) in African religions is to preserve the individual's well-being (through salvation). Thus salvation and liberation become a holistic individual-collective and personal-systemic ultimate concern.

In this theological anthropology African traditional religions also accent the role and importance of the ancestors. The ancestors are connections to the past religious traditions and practices. They are the glue to the sacredness of culture or way of life. Oftentimes one would have to placate the ancestors in order to reach the High God. So connectedness (or lack of connectedness) to those who hold religio-cultural deposits has grave implications regarding one's relation to the Divine. For my purposes, the cultural significance of the ancestors' role is the most relevant. The memory and presence of the ancestors helped preserve and teach the cultural heritage of the community. To be human-in-community necessitated a cultural dimension in African traditional religions.

Furthermore, enslaved Africans brought with them a sense of wholeness in the High God's relation to creation. Because God created all things, there was no separation between the sacred and secular, the church and the community.

> A sense of wholeness of the person is manifested in the African attitude to life. Just as there is no separation between the sacred and the secular in communal life, neither is there a separation between the soul and the body in a person. Spiritual needs are as important for the body as bodily needs are for the soul.[9]

One does not dichotomize God's sovereignty in any sphere. African traditional religions did not see the possibility of saving the spirit or the soul while the freedom of the body went unattended.[10]

BUSH ARBOR THEOLOGY

Enslaved Africans took the remnants of their traditional religious structures and meshed them together with their interpretation of the Bible. All this occurred in the "Invisible Institution," far away from the watchful eyes of white people. Only in their own cultural idiom and political space could black slaves truly worship God. Ex-slave Becky Ilsey describes the hidden nature of the "Invisible Institution" pre-Civil War: " 'Fo de war when we'd have a meetin' at night, wuz mos' always 'way in de woods or de bushes some whar so de white folks couldn't hear."[11] Slaves would sneak off "twixt eight an' twelve at night"[12] to hold church. At times, slaves sought whatever shelter they could find for their sanctuary in order "to talk wid Jesus." They "used to go 'cross de fields nights to a old tobacco barn on de side of a hill."[13]

If they found no standing shelter they would construct a bush (or hush) arbor for their illegal prayer meetings. Ex-slave Arthur Greene remembers:

> Well-er talkin' 'bout de church in dem days, we po' colored people ain' had none lak you have now. We jes made er bush arbor by cutin' bushes dat was full of green leaves an' puttin' em on top of four poles reachin' from pole to pole. Den sometimes we'd have dem bushes put roun' to kiver de sides an' back from der bottom to der top. All us get together in dis arbor fer de meetin'.[14]

Other times slaves secretly gathered in an appointed cabin in the slave quarters. "Niggers have benches in dey house dat dey use when dey have prayer-meetin's."[15] Some ingeniously set up worship spots in the fields ("Dey hab big holes out in de fiel's dey git down in and pray."). Some developed regular praying grounds. "Us niggers used to have a prayin' ground down in the hollow," remembers Richard Carruthers. And Andrew Moss echoes: "Us colored folks had prayer grounds. My mammy's was a old twisted thick-rooted muscadine bush." And still others would simply "slip down the hill" to worship.[16]

In the "Invisible Institution," the slaves displayed a remarkable clarity concerning the cultural dimension of their theology. They knew that God spoke to them in their own medium. In fact, African American chattel could not worship God truthfully unless they "talked" with God through their black culture. Ex-slave Emily Dixon makes it plain:

> Us could go to de white folk's church [in a segregated section], but us wanted ter go whar us could sing all de way through, an' hum 'long, an' shout—yo' all know, jist turn loose lack.

In slave religious culture the liberating Spirit made one "jist turn loose lack." The Spirit fed the slaves and instructed them on how to communicate with God using their own indigenous resources. "We used to steal off to de woods and have church, like de Spirit moved us—sing and pray to our own liking and soul satisfaction," states Susan Rhodes. Her testimony exemplifies the slaves' need to be filled with the spirit to their *own* liking and soul satisfaction. And when they claimed their relation to God through the Spirit's pouring into their unique expressions, Rhodes resumes, "we sure did have good meetings, honey . . . like God said."[17]

Like their self-expression in the cultural sphere, slaves acknowledged that their religious worship and theological development meant a political fight to preserve the "Invisible Institution." White folks not only passed laws to prevent African American bondsmen and bondswomen from receiving unsupervised religious instructions, but they also sought to whip and kill slaves who met secretly to praise God. Thus the "Invisible Institution" symbolized both a cultural statement of slave theology and a liberated space in which slaves controlled the political power to develop their theology.

To fight white folks politically—to claim and worship in their own space of sacred power—blacks devised various stratagems to conceal the "Invisible Institution." Minnie Folkes remembers: "So to keep de soun' from goin' out, slaves would put a gra' big iron pot at de do'." Katie Blackwess Johnson concurs: "I would see them 'turn down the pots' to keep the folks at the big-house from hearin' them singin' and prayin'."[18] Yet the whites proved relentless in imposing their theology on the slaves and attempting to squash the bondservants' political struggle to "hold church." Whites sent out "patrollers" to make bed checks in the slave shacks and to comb the woods to stifle the "Invisible Institution." Consequently, slaves responded with "lookouts" as decoys to confuse the patrollers. West Turner testifies, "Well, dey made me de lookout boy, an' when de paddyrollers [the patrollers] come down de lane past de church . . . well, sir, dey tell me to step out f'm de woods an' let 'em see me." The patrollers chased after Turner, who led them into a booby trap. Turner continues:

> Dem ole paddyrollers done rid plumb into a great line of grape vines dat de slaves had stretched 'cross de path. An' dese vines tripped up de horses an' throwed de ole paddyrollers off in de bushes.[19]

Turner's eyewitness account of the slaves' illegal church gatherings indicates a virtual political guerrilla warfare. Similarly, the picturesque story of former slave Rev. Ishrael Massie attests to the expression of slave religion in the "Invisible Institution" as hand-to-hand combat over who would have power to control the theology of the oppressed African Americans. Rev. Massie underscores this point:

> Lemme tell ya dis happenin' at a meetin'. Ole preacher would come in bringing . . . a long knot of lightwood. . . . When de paterrolers knock at de dow . . . dis preacher would run to de fiah place, git him a light an' take dat torch an' wave hit back an' fo'th so dat de pitch an' fiah would be flyin' every which a way in dese paterrolers faces — you know dat burnt 'em.[20]

Clearly part of the black preacher's pastoral duties included waging a physical war against white "principalities and powers" on earth.

To sum up, in the development of the political and cultural dimensions of the "Invisible Institution," the preacher and his or her following had no other choice but to steal away and "call on the name of the Lord" without fear of white power's lethal presence. Two factors brought this about: the proscriptions of white Christian theology, and the slaves' faith in God's partiality to the poor.

WHITE CHRISTIANITY

White theology forced its domination upon black life by ruthlessly controlling and rendering slaves subservient to white humanity. First, the *practice* of white slave masters' Christianity restricted African Americans' access to an independent encounter with religion. For instance, in those cases where whites allowed blacks to attend church, slaves experienced segregation in seating. Samuel Walter Chilton recalls: "Colored folks had to set in de gallery. Dey [white Christians] didn' 'low dem to take part in service." Similarly Caroline Hunter's former slave master would not permit slaves to enter the church sanctuary. A white man would preach to them in the basement of the church building. And Mr. Beverly Jones confirms: " 'Couse they wouldn' let us [slaves] have no services lessen a white man was present. Most times the white preacher preached. . . . That was the law at that time."[21]

In addition to legal restrictions in worship, the everyday practice of white Christianity displayed no ethical difference between "Christian" whites and non-Christian whites. The white master of ex-slave Jack White was a "Mef'dis preacher" who whipped his blacks just as often and just as cruelly as other white people did. To intensify the pain and heinousness of the lashing, this preacher would "drap pitch an' tuppentine on dem [the slaves' welts] from a bu'nin' to'ch." Another white preacher intentionally put out any fires built by his slaves during the winter. As a result, his bondservants "et frozen meat and bread many times in cold weather." And maintaining the tradition of white Christianity's practical barbarity, this particular preacher soaked the raw whipping wounds of his slaves in a "salt bath."[22]

Summarizing the slaves' perspective of white Christianity's daily brutalities, former bondswoman Mrs. Joseph Smith offers this succinct and insightful conclusion:

> Those who were Christians [and] held slaves were the hardest masters. A card-player and drunkard wouldn't flog you half to death. Well, it is something like this—the Christians will oppress you more.[23]

Besides the practice of white slave masters' Christianity, white theology sought to control and make black people slaves to its *doctrinal propositions*. The uncivilized witness and ethics of whites were not simply aberrations from their faith claims about God. On the contrary, white folks literally practiced what they preached. Their *theology* itself propagated white control and black subservience as the normative expression of the Christian gospel.

The slave narratives overflow with white theological justifications for the "peculiar institution." First, the worship leader "always took his text from Ephesians, the white preacher did, the part what said, 'Obey your masters, be good servants.' " Hence whites employed the authority of the Bible in a self-serving and racist interpretation. Having adopted this Pauline epistle as a standard homily, slave masters further construed a catechism for their black human property. "We had a catechism to learn," narrates Sister Robinson. "This wuz it: 'Be nice to massa an' missus, don't tell lies, don't be mean, be obedient an' wuk hard.' " Coupling this religious instruction with the following white man's sermon renders even more clearly the intricacies of slave-master theology. Quoting a white preacher, ex-slave Jenny Proctor restates:

> Now I takes my text, which is, Nigger obey your master and your mistress, 'cause what you git from them here in this world am all you ever going to git, 'cause you just like the hogs and the other animals—when you dies you ain't no more, after you been throwed in that hole.[24]

What does this tell us about white theological beliefs regarding black religious humanity? Whites viewed slaves like other livestock ("hogs and the other animals"). Therefore God had created them and intended for them to work for their white masters with a cheerful and loyal countenance. Further, lacking any ultimate future of heavenly reward, slaves needed to rest content with the earthly constraints of bondage.

Finally, even if slave masters granted any possibility of slaves attaining the blessed repose of heaven, they had to beseech the white man as their Savior. For example, a slave master caught his slave praying and demanded that the slave explain to whom he offered supplications. The slave replied: "Oh Marster, I'se just prayin' to Jesus 'cause I wants to go to Heaven when I dies." Belligerently and arrogantly, the Marster replied, "You's my Negro. I get ye to Heaven."[25] Here we touch the heart of white Christianity and theology. The white man believed he filled the mediating and liberating role of Jesus Christ. As the anointed Jesus, the white man possessed omnipotent and salvific capabilities. For black chattel to reach God, then, whites forced African Americans to accept the status of the white race as divine mediator. However, black folks rejected these scurrilous and heretical faith claims.[26] Though physically bound, slaves nevertheless directly encountered the biblical God in their own theological creativity.

THE SLAVES' BLACK THEOLOGY

White theological proscriptions served as the negative incentive for slaves to pursue their independent religious thinking. On the positive side, blacks felt the powerful living presence of the Divine in the midst of their daily burdens and concentrated in the "Invisible Institution." These radical religious experiences colored their biblical interpretation, and thus they produced a theology of liberation. So far we have reviewed the various contours of the "Invisible Institution." Against that backdrop we can chart three manifestations of this liberation encounter with the slaves' black theological perspective on God, Jesus Christ, and humanity.

GOD

EXODUS: GOD HEARD OUR CRIES
African American bondsmen and bondswomen discovered their own predicament and deliverance in the story of the Old Testament Israelites, who also suffered bondage.

> All us had was church meetin's in arbors out in de woods. De preachers would exhort us dat us was de chillen o' Israel in de wilderness an' de Lord done sent us to take dis land o' milk and honey.[27]

And so they reached back into biblical times and appropriated Yahweh's promises and accomplishments for their contemporary dilemma. Paralleling the faith of the Israelites, ex-slave Henry Bibb wrote in his autobiography: "I never omitted to pray for deliverance. I had faith to believe that the Lord could see our wrongs and hear our cries."[28] Pursuing a theological journey from the Old Testament Yahweh to their current religious life with God, slaves directly experienced for themselves the mighty words of Yahweh: "I have surely seen the affliction of my people which are in Egypt and I have heard their cry. . . . And I am come down to deliver them" (Ex 3:1-8a). In this biblical paradigm American slaves discovered the *nature* of God as the One who sees the afflictions of the oppressed, hears their cries, and delivers them to freedom.

Despite white folks' prohibitions against learning to read the Bible and despite the apparent immortality of the slave system, black chattel persisted in a faith in the God of freedom. They combined remains from African traditional religions with the liberation message in the Bible and simply refused to accept white theology. John Bates fondly recalls: "My uncle, Ben, he could read de Bible, and he allus tell us some day us be free." Bates's statement signifies the slaves' unshakeable intellectual analysis and heartfelt belief that the *being* and *work* of God was liberation. Consequently, they incessantly prayed for deliverance.[29]

Indeed, for those in chains, God heard their cries.[30] God did not turn a deaf ear to such soul-wrenching supplications; neither did God ignore such "little ones" in distress. God displayed the *compassion* of a loving and caring parent with the inherent attribute of *agape* — an unflinching divine love for the poor. This knowledge of Yahweh-God's steadfast love empowered illiterate slave preachers to risk the pain of death in order to proclaim the word of God to a bush arbor "congregation."

An unidentified slave preacher remembers how he first began preaching by regurgitating the prescribed words of the slave master ("obeys the master"). Though lacking in literacy, this preacher nonetheless felt filled with God's Spirit, which moved him to contradict his previous sermon on subservience obliged by white theological doctrine ("I knowed there's something better for [the slaves]"). As a result, he felt compelled to proclaim the word of God "but daren't tell [the slaves] 'cept on the sly. That I done lots." Perhaps surreptitiously crowded deep in a damp ravine under the bright blackness of the midnight hour, this preacher in chains brought forth the good news to his brothers and sisters: "I tells 'em iffen they keeps praying, the Lord will set 'em free."[31] God hears and God frees.

More specifically, God freed the slaves in one decisive divine action — the Civil War. Various slave stories, accordingly, attrib-

ute the success of the Yankee forces over the Confederates to
God's will. Charles Grandy typifies this sentiment.

> Den a gra' big star over in de east come right down almos'
> to de earth. I seed it myself. 'Twas sign o' war alright.
> Niggers got glad. All dem what could pray 'gin to pray
> more 'n ever. So glad God sendin' de war.[32]

Like the Old Testament Yahweh, who sent natural signs before
freeing the Israelites, God disrupted the normal course of nature
with a "gra' big star" coming from the east as a sign of war. And
the poor became "so glad God sendin' de war." Clearly, for
African American chattel, God's compassion and *agape* did not
exclude a belligerent deed against the enemies of God's people.
Consistent with the biblical narrative and reflecting out of their
own story, slaves knew that divine pathos brought God to the
defense of victims of injustice. Because of love, the Divinity
resorts to a warlike nature. J. W. Lindsay believed "that perhaps
God means to bring good out of this great war. God is a man
of war, and Jehovah is his name."[33] The slaves, then, conjured
up theological images of Jehovah with arms outstretched leading
the victorious advance on the battlefield against the evil system
of slavery.

Yet the slaves did not restrict the image of God the Warrior
to the Civil War. They also linked this war notion against evil
and bondage to a holistic concept of God's mercy as a balm for
individual tribulations. In other words, God served the reliable
role of black people's total deliverer, both in the systemic and
in the personal realms. For instance, Ole Ant Sissy had suffered
from paralysis for numerous years. But when she heard of the
war's conclusion and the abolition of slavery, she "hobbled on
out de do', an stood dere prayin' to Gawd fo' his Mercy." Theologically, bondsmen and bondswomen coupled corporate freedom with personal healing. Note how the Good News of victory
through battle yields a cure for paralysis. "God is a momentary God" whose mercy can answer one's prayers in a mere
moment.[34]

WE HAVE A JUST GOD

The slaves' prayerful beseeching of God for deliverance indicates that they believed fundamentally that God's nature was one of justice and liberation. In fact, such a faith kept hope alive for these poor chattel, who groaned under the heel of a stultifying existence. All around them stood white Christians, taunting them with the supposedly biblically based and inherent superiority of white skin over black. Moreover, whites apparently had the military and intellectual power to implement this heretical claim of theological racism. But divine justice radically subverted the priority of white-skinned privileges in the slaves' sacred world-view. More specifically, with solemn certainty and joyful delight, blacks sang: "We have a just God to plead-a our cause/ We have a just God to plead-a our cause/We are the people of God./He sits in Heaven and he answers prayer."[35]

A just God brought righteousness in situations of conflict between the weak and the strong. For human property, righteousness corrected unjust relations and placed the Divinity squarely and unapologetically on the side of the oppressed. How could it be otherwise? Surely, since Yahweh heard their anguished cries and saw their cruel plight, Yahweh would "make things right." By bearing the innocent victims' burden, God stood with them and, furthermore, burst asunder systemic tentacles that literally choked the very lives of African American bondsmen and bondswomen. In an interview former slave James L. Bradley boldly declared: "God will help those who take part with the oppressed. Yes, blessed be His holy name! He will surely do it."[36] In a word, God sides with the downtrodden.

Conversely, God punishes the wicked. Understandably, the slaves believed in a theological formula of divine justice and righteousness in which the oppressor reaped the deserved condemnation. Black chattel underwent sadistic and savage treatment at the hands of fiendish white folks. Whites often gave slaves fifty to five hundred lashes and then poured salt, turpentine, or ground bricks into the fresh wounds. White males entered slave cabins and raped black women in the presence of their husbands. White males consistently "broke in" young black girls just arrived into puberty. Quite often slaves had their thumbs cut off for attempting to learn reading and writing. Slave traders purchased black women, snatched their children from their nursing breasts, and threw the babies on the side of the road to die. Death stalked the slaves like a bounty hunter dogging a fugitive. The slightest whim could set off the vicious nature of whites. In one instance a slave woman accidently spilled gravy on the white dress of a slave mistress. The master took the black woman outdoors and cut her head off.[37]

Hence, for the enslaved, the justice and righteousness of God could only bring retribution for tormentors. Julia Brown concurs: "When he died we all said God got tired of Mister Jim being so mean and kilt him." But divine establishment of right relations entailed even more chastisement for the offender. "God has whipped some of 'em worse dan dey beat us."[38] Even more, satisfaction for sinful and vicious acts against society's weak did not cease with the slave masters. It resumed with and haunted their descendants. Drawing on all of his theological knowledge and religious experience, former slave the Rev. Ishrael Massie asserted: "God's gwine punish deir chillun's chillun, yas sur!"[39]

Similarly, slaves juxtaposed God's justice with the kingdom of God. In fact, they perceived institutional slavery as a struggle between two kingdoms—that of God and that of Satan. Not surprisingly, the white master was Satan's proxy and belonged to his domain. The fruits of the master's earthly labor, then, yielded a permanent dwelling in hell. "I ain' plannin' on meetin' him in heaven," says a slave about her master. The fact that "Marse was an' ole Methodist preacher" would not prevent his arrival in the flames of hell. Others claimed that their masters were so mean they "went past heaven."[40]

Not only did a biblical interpretation of divine sovereignty inform bondservants about the masters' demonic kingdom, white practice gave credence to such a belief. When white patrollers happened upon the secret worship services of the "Invisible Institution," they inevitably whipped slaves fresh from prayer. As white hands ferociously gripped bullwhips and broke the exposed skin of bent black backs, the patrollers mocked God and claimed: "Ef I ketch you heah agin servin' God, I'll beat you. You havn' time to serve God. We bought you to serve us." Based on black folks' reading of Christian scriptures, all who opposed God served Satan. And when one master arrogantly proclaimed, "The Lord rule Heaven, but [I] Jim Smith rule the earth," slaves knew to which kingdom they belonged.[41]

To belong to God's realm meant African American chattel professed themselves children of God, who promised that they, the meek, should inherit the earth. Like Israel, if God owned them in God's sacred domain, they held the deed to a land of milk and honey. For the God of deliverance would fulfill the divine promise to God's possessions. Under slavery the children of God secretly hoped for the day of Jubilee, the inbreaking of God's Kingdom on earth. In fact, when "the walls came tumbling down" with God's Civil War, former chattel could "jist turn loose lack" and speak the truth. If previously they practiced stealth and ambiguity in theological imagery, now they plainly proclaimed. While former white masters slithered into hiding at the sound of advancing cannon fire, former slaves joyously jumped for Jubilee. They cried out with a renewed spirit and an open, defiant chorus:

> Old massa run away
> And us darkies stay at home.
> It must be now dat Kingdom's comin'
> And de year of Jubilee.[42]

Finally, the issue of the black slaves' perception of God (king-dom-coming talk) in contrast to the white masters' faith is, in the most fundamental and profound sense, a theological debate about the nature of God. One ex-slave tells a story about a white minister who, more than likely, preached the standard "slaves obey your master" sermon to the blacks on the plantation. Uncle Silas, a 100-year-old slave, hobbled up to the front row and challenged the white preacher with a pointed inquiry: "Is us slaves gonna be free in Heaven?" The preacher abruptly halted his religious instructions and eyed Uncle Silas with vile contempt and a desire to kill him for questioning white theological doc-trine. However, Uncle Silas did not budge and this time resumed the debate with a yell: "Is God gonna free us slaves when we git to Heaven?" The white preacher withdrew a handkerchief, mopped the sweat from his pale white brow and replied, "Jesus says come unto Me ye who are free fum sin an' I will give you salvation." Undaunted Uncle Silas rebutted: "Gonna give us freedom 'long wid salvation?" The preacher resumed his homily and Uncle Silas remained standing up front during the rest of the service.[43] Uncle Silas epitomizes the millions of blacks under slavery who refused to accept white people's notion of God, that is, that blacks were to serve whites and maybe receive some amorphous reward after death. On the one hand stood a white male, symbolizing theological degrees, recognized Christian ordination, patriarchy, racial privilege, economic power, and Satan. On the other stood Uncle Silas, poor, black, unlettered, and a child of God.

For Uncle Silas, and the slaves, the debate revolved around the nature of God's liberation, the nature of the in-breaking of God's kingdom. Above all, Yahweh brought freedom; without it personal salvation proved an opiate of the oppressed. Note that Uncle Silas does not deny the fruit of individual salvific power. What he wants to know and what he *demands* to know is whether or not individual release from sin intersected with the radical overthrow of a racist system of injustice. What does God have to say about that? From the vantage point of chattel, we have seen how God embodies the Exodus, realizes justice for the marginalized, and brings God's children into the Kingdom.

JESUS

JESUS WON'T DIE NO MORE

In the above story the white preacher attempted to undermine the pressing theological queries of Uncle Silas by bastardizing Jesus' promise of salvation. Still, Uncle Silas remained undeterred and vigorously pressed the question of Jesus' salvation in relation to liberation. This surfaces the slaves' interpretation of Jesus' role in their overall theological construct.

Deeply rooted in the Old Testament Scriptures, black people linked Jesus to Israel's fate and, consequently, underscored the ultimate and decisive dimension of divine presence. The following spiritual confirms this assertion:

> Jesus said He wouldn't die no mo',
> Said He wouldn't die no mo',

> So my dear chillens don' yer fear,
> Said He wouldn't die no mo'.
>
> De Lord tole Moses what ter do,
> Said He wouldn't die no mo',
> Lead de chillen ob Isr'el froo',
> Said He wouldn' die no mo'.[44]

It is clear that slaves positioned Jesus in the time of Moses. "De Lord tole Moses what ter do" indicates that Jesus had become Moses' contemporary. Because bondservants anchored themselves in the great deliverance achievements of Yahweh and the story of the oppressed Israelites, their sense of divine time did not restrict itself to a linear progression of God's inter-action in human affairs. In fact, far from being a whimsical interpretation of the Bible, black folks' retro-projection of Jesus to Moses' days reflects an authentic and faithful reading of scripture. The slaves correctly followed the instructions from the prologue of John's gospel, which didactically states: "In the beginning was the Word and the Word was with God." If the Word, who is Jesus, existed in the beginning of time, then surely Jesus had the ability and the power to exhort Moses during the latter's time.

However, the appearance of Jesus during Moses' time speaks about more than human time. In addition and more fundamentally, the above quoted spiritual pinpoints the divine time of *kairos* — the divine importance of Jesus' earthly mission of liberation. The constant refrain of Jesus never dying anymore underlines the momentous significance of Jesus' death and resurrection for humankind, particularly the prototype oppressed Israel. Why the heavy emphasis on "die no mo' "? Because Jesus defeated the kingdom of Satan and all the political forces of evil representative of the demonic in all realms. Jesus won't "die no mo' " because there is no need for a future divine intermediary to conquer the political demons of evil powers. For the black chattel, then, the liberating nature of Jesus dying meant a radical alteration witnessed by Jesus initiating the kingdom.

At the same time that we fathom the import of Jesus' death, we must be careful not to miss the slaves' conscious interplay between the liberation motif of poor oppressed Israel in the Old Testament and the liberation motif of Jesus in the New Testament. Positioning Jesus back with Moses did not mean that black folks made relative or negated the earth-shattering divide between the political power of Satan and that of Jesus realized by the latter's earthly appearance (in the New Testament). On the contrary, by stationing Jesus back with Moses, the entire Exodus event becomes a paradigmatic foreshadowing of the liberation consequences of Jesus' death and resurrection—the universal poor's grand exodus from poverty to freedom. The slaves were radically centered on Jesus.

In a sense, Israel's rough wilderness journey and ultimate victory in Canaan mirrored Jesus' cross-resurrection experience. The interweaving of the Israel story with Jesus not dying anymore points to the slaves' claim of such a theological parallel. The One Jesus, noted for a sacrificial emptying-suffering and resurrection-glorification, acted as the freedom Word in Israel's suffering and eventual "glorification." Placing Jesus during the time when Moses led the first cross-resurrection journey, the first covenant, prepares the slaves for and confirms the omnipotent, liberating, and irresistible grace of the cross-resurrection event, that is, the final covenant. Jesus had a hand in the movement of Israel; when Jesus died, Jesus would never "die no mo' '" because the cross-resurrection event symbolized the finality of satanic powers' absolute rout. Moreover, the constant emphasis on "die no mo'" sounds a note of confidence, courage, and hope for the blacks in bondage—"So my dear chillens don' yer fear." There is no need to fear the earthly white power structure. Since Jesus, through Moses, led the exploited Israelite people to victory and finished off Satan with the Cross and Resurrection, no human advocates for the Devil could defeat Jesus' just cause of black people's struggle for liberation.

The ultimate goal of Jesus' liberation movement by necessity must lead to freedom because the very being of Jesus is freedom. The following famous slave spiritual defines this ontological character.

> Steal away, steal away,
> Steal away to Jesus,

> Steal away, steal away home,
> I hain't got long to stay here.

In this instance, slaves employed a double meaning as a communication code to deceive paranoid whites ever on the lookout for religiously inspired slave rebellions. Such disguised slave songs heralded a distinct slave language. Thus even in their culture, bondsmen and bondswomen spoke of Jesus in their own linguistic modality. Black folk related to one another in a religious cultural medium that befuddled the normative white English and circumvented standard (white) morphology. Accordingly, in certain instances "Steal Away" utilized Jesus to represent a secret prayer meeting of the "Invisible Institution." In other cases Jesus stood for passage on Harriet Tubman's Underground Railroad to Canada or up North. For the Rev. Nat Turner, a black Baptist preacher, "Steal Away to Jesus" symbolized the gathering of his prophetic band of Christian witnesses in preparation for armed struggle and guerrilla warfare against slavery.[45] Regardless of the usage of "Jesus" in black slave English—whether a free space; or a meeting to strategize for freedom; or freedom in heaven, the land of milk and honey in the cultural language of African American chattel—the essential being of Jesus is freedom.

JESUS' OFFICES AND ATTRIBUTES

In addition to ascribing ultimate significance and liberation ontology to Jesus, slaves also experienced specific offices in Jesus in particular, the kingly and priestly offices.[46] King Jesus imaged a conquering hero, a valiant warrior defiantly and triumphantly situated upon his majestic stallion. Given the slaves' lowly and persecuted existence, nothing could better picture the kingly office than a mighty and royal warrior. Slaves, therefore, sang from the depths of hearts that yearned for the King to come upon his stead as the Liberator. "Ride on, King Jesus," cry out the lyrics of one spiritual, "Ride on, conquering King."[47] Another verse describes Jesus and Satan: "King Jesus ride a milk-white horse," whereas "Satan ride an iron-gray horse." The slaves made their Jesus theology explicit; the Warrior King fought Satan, king of another kingdom. Because Jesus brought the Good News of ultimate deliverance and revealed a being of liberation, King Satan stood for all that prevented freedom. For black chattel, King Satan's earthly domain was the slavery system, which would inevitably succumb to the Conquering King.

The kingly office linked directly to the priestly office of Jesus in another slave spiritual.

> King Jesus lit de candle by de waterside,
> To see de little chillun when dey truly baptize.
> Honor! Honor unto de dying Lamb.
>
> Oh, run along chillun, an be baptize
> Might pretty meetin' by de waterside.
> Honor! Honor! unto de dying Lamb.[48]

Here the Conquering King serves as pastor over the "Invisible Institution," "pretty meetin' by de waterside." In the office of priest Jesus officiates at the baptismal rituals, initiating the religious service by lighting the candles. Secretly gathered at a stream or brook around midnight, black chattel called on the Lord to preside over their ceremony of dying and rising again through the process of full immersion, that is, "when dey truly baptize." Quite fittingly, just as Jesus had died and risen again—and thus become a new person—the slaves wanted to experience that same manifestation of new life in the presence of the One who was born again so that they too might be free in the New Being of Jesus. Coupled with the ontological essence of Jesus, baptism in the presence of the priestly Jesus signified deliverance from the earthly snares of sin and oppression. Therefore, to become new a slave died and buried the old self of subservience and attachment to sin-slavery and raised up the new self from the baptismal waters into salvation-liberation before the Priest. To be in Jesus is to be in freedom.

One also has to grasp the significance of the "dying Lamb" metaphor in the spiritual. Jesus offered Jesus' self as the paradigmatic sacrifice on the altar for the welfare of all humankind by spilling blood and dying. Quite conscious of this theological and cosmological priestly function, slaves, accordingly, give "Honor! unto de dying Lamb," and they run along to partake of the results of the Lamb's death by plunging themselves in the baptismal waters. One honors the Lamb by imitation and by service. Hence, under the loving eye of the priestly Jesus, slave baptism marked both a religious ceremonial and theological rite of passage. Reflecting their correct grasp of the Christian Scriptures, the slaves knew that the blood of the Lamb washes one clean of all sin through the ritual of baptism and, at the same time, the dying Lamb shifts the new person forever into the domain of Jesus, hence a theological transformation.

Besides the kingly and priestly offices, slaves acknowledged certain personal attributes of Jesus in the role of friend, converter, and mother. Slaves deeply cherished friendship. Friendship did not simply hold a status of casual acquaintance; quite the opposite, it literally brought either life or death. For example, the religious rebellions led by Denmark Vesey and Gabriel Prosser against slavery were both imperilled and then betrayed by obsequious slaves subservient to white theological idolatry. The denial of friendship resulted in black men and women losing their lives in these aborted religious uprisings.[49] Understandably, slaves attributed the supreme title of friend to Jesus, the One who never would forsake you in trials and tribulations. Black folk sang with confidence:

> Old Satan is one busy ole man;
> He rolls dem blocks all in my way;
> But Jesus is my bosom friend;
> He rolls dem blocks away.[50]

There is some ambiguity about the nature of Satan's "blocks" in this particular spiritual. But one can understand that, because slaves labored in the cotton fields and sang these lines in the presence of the white master, they wanted to allow enough ambiguity in the words to keep Ole Massa from detecting their full meaning. Out of necessity slaves developed a deceptive linguistic culture of survival to subvert white discovery of genuine slave thought. But when this spiritual burst forth from the prayerful lips of black folk in the "Invisible Institution," their own sacred political and cultural space, Satan distinctly and most definitely denoted slavery and the evils of white people. For the slaves

Jesus, the bosom friend, ceaselessly and consistently destroyed the "blocks" of the devilish slave system and thereby thwarted death and preserved black life.

In the second personal attribute, Jesus as Converter dynamically holds together individual and communal, sacred and secular salvation-liberation. When Jesus entered their lives for the first time, slaves sensed a profound turning away from sin and evil and a turning toward Jesus. Black folks named this process conversion, the movement toward the divine in Jesus. To partake of salvation, therefore, one underwent a conversion experience. Fannie Moore relates this testimony of her mother immediately after the elder's conversion engagement with Jesus:

> I'se saved. De Lord done tell me I'se saved. Now I know de Lord will show me de way, I ain't gwine to grieve no more. No matter how much you all done beat me and my chillen de Lord will show me de way. And some day we never be slaves.[51]

When Jesus converts a person, he or she no longer can live and see in the old manner. Jesus communicates directly and instructs the convert that past sins have been washed away and that the person has been set on a new path. This new direction of salvation, this new journey or way, provides certainty about future liberation and a radically new vision about upcoming events in both individual and collective life. The above conversion witness imparts such a definite faith in the new life that, with the Word of Jesus, even whippings and severe punishment cannot deter the proclamation of the hope of good news to come.

Certainly the conversion process first frees Fannie Moore's mother from grievance and heavy burdens. Indeed, her personal transformation gives her nothing but joy and hope in those things not yet seen but promised; Jesus frees her personally. But glad tidings do not restrict themselves to one individual. The mother rejoices not only because Jesus has given her strength to bear torment and distress, but also because, having met Jesus, she knows that "trouble won't last always"; that is, slavery will soon perish and all things will be made new in the Lord's time.

She joins personal salvation with the future redemption of the entire black community; she links her own existential sacred release with the total deliverance of the community. Harking back to her African cosmological nexus between sacred and secular as well as accurately building from the biblical intertwining of religious and "non-religious," a converted slave cannot shout for joy unless that joy encompasses deliverance for oppressed humankind.

Resuming the story, Fannie Moore describes her mother in this manner: "My mammy just grin all over her black wrinkled face." Though her face is jet black, with all the consequent negative and deleterious implications conjured up under slavery, Mammy nonetheless experienced the future vision of earthly liberation granted to her by Jesus' grace in conversion. Not even the whip of the slave master prevented Mammy from rejoicing in the Lord always for what the Lord had done for her. Jesus set her on the straight and narrow way. And even when the cowhide lashes ripped the skin off of her back, she "just go back to de field a singin'." Neither the bullwhip nor the backbreaking labor could stop her melodious voice from rising to heaven. No doubt she sang with renewed theological clarity and energy such sentiments as: "I don't feel weary and noways tired" and "Good news, member, good news, And I hearde from heav'n today."[52]

The image of Jesus as mother, the third and last personal attribute, evolves in the following spiritual:

> I heard the voice of Jesus callin'
> Come unto me and live.
> Lie, lie down, weepin' one,
> Rest thy head on my breast.
> I come to Jesus as I was,
> Weary and lone and tired and sad,
> I finds in him a restin' place,
> And he has made me glad.[53]

Weighted down with aches and pains caused by forced labor (which yielded absolute profit for whites), black human property struggled to maintain some sense of physical relief and spiritual nourishment. No earthly force could provide an adequate "restin' place"; Jesus could. Slaves needed suckling and nurturing; Jesus bestowed both. Jesus, exhibiting maternal qualities, beckoned them to "rest thy head on my breast," a secure place where those in bondage could relax in the warmth and renewing milk of divine comfort. A mother's sustenance supplies all the physical, intellectual, and spiritual support required to fend off the "troubles of de world," so that Jesus' little children could survive the lethal snares of Satan on their journey down the straight and narrow path. Yes, conversion enabled one to turn away from the vicious entrapments of the sinful slavery system (for example, not succumb to the false omnipotence of white folks) and pursue the righteousness of a new way. But conversion did not completely remove one from the brutal realities of the white man's rawhide whip. Rather, to maintain a faithful and liberated mind, spirit, and body, one needed to lean on the Lord.

Thus Jesus extended outstretched arms and offered the manna of life: "Come unto me and live." A child of the Lord needed only to come to Jesus, just as any child would approach his or her loving parent for restoration and vivifying renewal. For the poor, all the world says No!, but Jesus calls the earth's downtrodden to lie in the cradle of divine arms. Jesus offers soothing solace and acceptance for the weary, tired, and sad. Summoned from the cotton, sugarcane, or tobacco fields after eighteen hours of work, whipped with one hundred stripes from a cat-o-nine tails, soul crushed when one's babies were sold to the highest bidder, repeatedly raped by white slave masters and their sons, who together forced entrance into black women's slave cabins,[54] intellectually assaulted by laws forbidding the teaching of reading and writing to slaves, and kicked into the "nigger box" for several weeks because white people wanted to "break them down," black chattel needed and craved the loving and salutary breast of Jesus, the Mother, who "made me glad."

Jesus' offices and attributes brought joy because slaves rightly perceived an incarnational divine purpose that not only privileged the lowly social location of poor blacks but also marshalled all of creation for their ultimate deliverance. Rev. Bentley, a black Baptist preacher, recounts a sermon he once gave to his co-bondservants before emancipation.

I remember on one occasion, when the President of the United States came to Georgia ... the president came in a grand, beautiful carriage and drove to the best house in the whole town. ... But a cord was drawn around the house to keep us negroes and other poor folks from coming too near. ... But the great gentlemen and the rich folks went freely up the steps and in through the door and shook hands with him.

Rev. Bentley draws from the depths of his slave theological knowledge and convictions in order to paint an accurate picture of Jesus' sole incarnational intent. On the one side, he distinguishes the president enveloped in all the amenities of opulence and eminent stature. The president of the United States, archetypal political figurehead, holds the reins of the white power structure. The president assumes his commander-in-chief status at the behest of the nation's wealthy. Boasting the best of white, slave-master Christianity, he struts about under the mantle of absolute prestige with a sense of authoritative erudition like a king before his subjects. He epitomizes the sacred bearer of white culture and language; he depicts the pinnacle of male dominance in society. The president surrounds himself with wealth and those of his ilk: a grand beautiful carriage, the best white house, and the company of the rich white folks.

On the other hand, Rev. Bentley indicates a theological divide symbolized by the "cord." The cord symbolizes slavery, a rope used to whip and hang blacks, a barrier to forcefully lock out the poor African Americans from the earth's riches, which they have labored to create. Unlike the rich white folks, blacks huddle at the bottom of the steps to the wealthy white house; they cannot "freely" enter anywhere. They have no grand carriage or fine horses, and they never shake the president's hand. They lack decent clothing, adequate food, and sufficient shelter. The cord serves to rope them in and press them to the plow like the harness around a mule's neck. The cord wraps around their mind and spirit to stunt their theological and emotional development. The cord hides and confines them in the dinginess of the slave quarters. They cannot be seen or heard; they cannot plead their cases before earthly "royalty." White people have

given them the gift of slavery and a rope, not liberation.
Then Rev. Bentley resumes his sermon:

> Now, did Christ come in that way? Did he come only to
> the rich? ... No! Blessed be the Lord! He came to the
> poor! He came to us, and for our sakes![55]

Indeed, from the viewpoint of those at the bottom of the
steps, Jesus Christ incarnated Jesus' self in the condition of
poverty. Was not Jesus born in a manger amid cow dung because
the powerful "capitalist" owner of the inn refused admission to
wealthless strangers like Mary and Joseph? Did not Jesus
become homeless, forced to wander in the back alleys of this
world, "no place to lay his head"? Jesus too had been hunted
like a criminal and outcast by the bloodhounds and rulers of his
day. Had not the official theologians and religious leaders
mocked and scorned Jesus' scriptural interpretations? And
finally, did Jesus not endure whipping and a bloodied body
pierced by nails to a wooden cross like the black ones lynched
from a sagging tree on white folks' plantations? Rev. Bentley
preached a theology that resonated with his slave congregation.
With rustic but sophisticated clarity he apprehended the divine
self-emptying into the human Jesus among squalor ("He came
to the poor!"), and he knew that Jesus with all of God's creation
came "for our sakes." Jesus Christ materialized for the poor and
intended liberation for the poor. Hence Jesus delivers the gospel
of incarnational divine purpose for human freedom.

HUMANITY

CREATED IN FREEDOM

Perceptions of God and Jesus paved the way for the slaves'
notion of a God-given humanity; they knew they were created
in freedom. White theology and white Christian ethical practices
notwithstanding, black folk maintained they were not livestock
but infused from inception with inherent human attributes fashioned by divine hands. Former slave Charlie Moses sums up this
belief in theological anthropology: "God Almighty never meant
for human beings to be like animals. Us niggers has a soul an'

a heart an' a mine. We ain't like a dog or horse."[56] The omnipotence of divine creation decried white heretical faith claims and produced black people as God's possessions, fully equipped with necessary and sufficient qualities and resources to function in a liberated manner. Though enslaved, bondsmen and bondswomen believed that God brought them into this world with souls that allowed them to express their spirituality and religious experience with the Holy. Likewise, God gave them hearts to beat with the feelings and emotions that characterize human capabilities in situations of pathos and exhilaration. They were not callous labor items. And God provided them with "a mine" to think independently and rationally about theological phenomenan in relation to their full hearts and spirit-filled souls.

A soul signified a space for the Spirit to enter and transform black chattels' servile pariah status. A heart offered a receptacle for the divine compassion for liberation. And a mind proved vital in systematizing the black-God encounter so that the slaves' struggle for liberation was not simply a spontaneous and random assault against the heights of white power, but a deliberate and cohesive sacred world-view marching with the Spirit's warmth and God's passion for justice. To know in one's mind the freedom of God's liberation movement likewise entailed the feeling of the spiritual warmth in one's conversion process from the grip of sinful racism and toward the straight and narrow path of righteousness. Moreover, to have this knowledge meant that one possessed the emotional capability and intellectual gift to contrast the former non-converted, enslaved self with a renewed zest for deliverance.

Black folk felt deeply about their God-given humanity; none yearned to be a "dog or horse"; they sought to be liberated persons. Once planted on free soil, James L. Bradley speaks the truth about his former slave colleagues: "How strange it is that anybody should believe any human being could be a slave, and yet be contented!" Bradley strikes at the heart of white theological anthropology. Whites believe that blacks want to be and enjoy being subservient to white power. This basic fallacy lies in white people interpreting themselves as normative for black human self-definition. This view posits, at worst, an inherent lowly status to black attempts to handle major theological issues of the heart, soul, and mind and, at best, showers empty, false praises on black theological endeavors that attempt to imitate and, thereby, hopefully become white. Contrary to white folks' notions of black humanity, Bradley responds with the true image of African American humanity endowed with divine virtues when he proclaims: "I was never acquainted with a slave, however well he was treated, who did not long to be free."[57]

Black people longed to be free because they possessed not an ingrained lowliness or willingness toward a white mindset but an inherent and natural gravitation toward freedom. An irrepressible longing to be free engulfed black humanity. In his autobiography Henry Bibb describes this irresistible divine impulse: "It kindled a fire of liberty within my breast which has never yet been quenched." Thus in the very definition of black humanity, the yearning for liberation burned like a prairie fire, swift and wide. And nothing, neither white supremacy nor theological heresy, could put out this flame sparking slaves to achieve their God-intended full creativity. Bibb believes that the fire of resistance is part of his nature. Furthermore, he finds proofs of divine liberation for humankind in what he terms "the inevitable laws of nature's God." He concludes the necessity for black liberation from two divinely created sources: from the natural disposition of slaves (in contrast to their existential disposition) the heat of deliverance never wanes or subsides, even after attaining freedom; and from the tug of liberation manifest in God's creation of nature, whose laws display the foundational beauty of inevitable liberty unfettered by human constraints. Echoing the slaves' heart-soul-mind human paradigm, which whites named treason, Bibb concludes: "I could see that the All-wise Creator, had made man a free, moral, intelligent and accountable being."[58]

This subversiveness in black chattels' paradigm of theological anthropology grew out of their use of the intellect from the poor's perspective. They knew that humanity spells liberty. Hence slaves constantly had to struggle with unraveling the false theological consciousness existentially imposed by white definition (the slaves' temporary predicament) and the natural primordial gift from God (the slaves' created humanity). One can observe the slaves' wrestling with these two contradictory states of being in the theological testimony of ex-slave Thomas Likers.

> But as soon as I came to the age of maturity, and could think for myself, I came to the conclusion that God never meant me for a slave, [and] that I should be a fool if I didn't take my liberty if I got the chance.[59]

Once reaching religious intellectual maturity and thinking for himself without the forbidding noose of white religious catechism, homily, or doctrine, Likers discovered a whole new world of liberation, no doubt in the Bible, nature, and in himself. Like his fellow slaves' post-conversion, he perceived a three-part movement of human transformation. In part one the Divine had originally molded him out of nothing into freedom; in the second part, the white man had refashioned and skewed his given nature into the warped satanic system of slavery. But, upon reaching theological adulthood, Likers felt beckoned to participate with God (through Jesus Christ) in the re-creation of himself along the natural intent of unchained humanity. To act as God's copartner in the third phase of divinely inspired re-created humanity, Likers had to take his liberty through the resistance of politics and the culture of resistance.

RESISTANCE OF POLITICS

Through the grace of the ultimate paradigmatic New Humanity of Jesus Christ, attaining the fully re-created African American self required political resistance. In this regard slaves showed ingenuity, courage, and creativity. God called them to pursue a human life in opposition to unbridled white power. Accordingly, they devised means and mechanisms for combating slave forces of evil; they resisted individually and collectively for their free humanity. Individually, slaves ran away from plantation labor and overseer lashes. Such acts of defiance represented in microcosm slave insurrection by way of sporadic strikes, for African American chattel stood at the vortex of slavery's successful economic production. Likewise, uncompensated slave work built the infrastructure of the southern territory. Thus individual runaways launched continual sorties against the very underpinnings of white societal well-being when they refused to remain chattel — and instruments of production for white profit. Numerous slave interviews testify to black folks' assertion of humanity by speaking with their feet. Former slave Arthur Greene confirms these illegal departures from white plantations: "Lord, Lord! Yes indeed, plenty of slaves uster run away. Why dem woods was full o' 'em chile." Greene continues to describe a particular acquaintance of his who habited with nature to avoid reintroduction into slavery.

> I knowd one man dat took an' run away 'cause his master was so mean an' cruel. He lived in a cave in de groun' fer fifteen yeahs 'fo' Lee's surrender. He made himself a den under de groun'; he an' his wife, an' raised fifteen chillun down dar.[60]

In the wilderness one was immersed in God's manifestation of the divine laws of natural freedom. Above we discovered Henry Bibb's attestation of human freedom revealed to him in "inevitable laws of nature's God." The wilderness setting and nature tradition provided both a haven from white imposition of political power over black humanity as well as a communing with and reaffirmation of God's word of deliverance. Black people knew that Yahweh had brought the oppressed Israelite laborers out of Egypt into the wilderness on their way toward Canaan land. God had led them. And in this temporary sojourn of the Hebrew children Yahweh had provided manna from heaven. Apparently the biblical God also maintained and nourished the slave who dwelled in a cave for fifteen years. Not only did he survive off of the fruits of the wilderness, but God blessed him and his wife with their own lives and the lives of fifteen children. For them the wilderness experience supplied protection from ever present white eyes and assisted their free humanity with sustaining sustenance. Truly God could make a way out of no way for those who dared to claim their genuine humanity.

Dwelling in the woods, in a cave in the wilderness, individual contraband slaves, no doubt, sent their voices up to Jesus. One of their spirituals indicates this:

1. I sought . . . my Lord in de wilderness,
   [I seek my Lord] in de wilderness, in de wilderness;
   I sought . . . my Lord in de wilderness,
   For I'm a-going home.

2. I found . . . grace in the wilderness. . . .[61]

Why were the woods so full of runaways, slaves who defined their humanity as more than white folks' private property and no less than as free children of God? Because the One who offered freedom to oppressed humanity tarried there on the boundaries of society in opposition to the whitewashed columns of the slave masters' residences. Therefore African American bondservants sought to exist with the Lord Jesus, who had conquered Satan's evil hold on all humanity, in "de wilderness." Jesus' momentous victory empowered those who dared to reach out to receive the divine offer of liberation. In a word, slaves sought to bring to fruition the full potential of their humanity by making themselves available in the wilderness to Jesus' power to break burdensome yokes for deliverance. No wonder they shouted: "I found free grace in the wilderness." Wilderness grace freely offered by Jesus conveyed a calling and commission to realize African American freedom, free grace for human freedom.

Individual political resistance to the desecration of God's black humanity also showed in the slaves' tenacious acts of self-defense. Because God created them, slaves had faith that their very being contained deposits of divine presence, which compelled them to act in self-defense to preserve these infused life-sustaining deposits from the finger of God. In one example, an overseer severely lashed an old black woman for what he perceived as her slow plowing in the fields. In response, the slave woman took her work implement and defended herself. "The woman became sore [from the whipping] and took her hoe and chopped him right across his head, and, child, you should have seen how she chopped this man to a bloody death."

To attack slaves, then, equalled a demonic attack on their inherent Godness. One could not allow Satan's earthly devils to prevail over that which belonged to the kingdom of God. On the contrary, once converted to the path of God through Jesus, black chattel believed they were obligated to wage a battle against the evil forces that relentlessly and untiringly struggled to pull them back to the dominion of Satan's white representatives. In a similar situation, another overseer expressed his anger toward an Aunt Susie Ann and "beat her till the blood run off her on the ground." Aunt Susie feigned unconsciousness as she fell to the aggressor's feet, and after the white overseer had put away his whip Aunt Susie grabbed this weapon and "whips him till he couldn't stand up."[62] The slaves did not believe that God's children should suffer despoiling of their bodies—temples of God's creation—in order for them to clothe themselves again with the idolatrous raiments of sin. Therefore, black chattel had to draw an unyielding line of demarcation between their humanity, crafted by divinity, and a subservient self slaving beneath Satan's rule.

Nevertheless, from a practical standpoint, one black slave could not succeed against the monstrosity of the slavery institution. Nor was the African American definition of humanity limited to an individual's singular rebellious nature. In fact, the resistance of politics connected individual opposition to communal insurrectionary support; one person succeeded in achieving full humanity only when the community aided in the deliverance process. Individual black humanity was manifested fully in relation to and in the context of a larger African American communal humanity. "Runaways use to come to our house all de time," relates former slave Mollie Booker, "to git somepin to eat." No one person, no matter how self-reliant, could sustain himself or herself in an absolute condition of isolation from the protective eyes and ears of fellow slaves if he or she wished to succeed in political resistance.

In certain cases the shrewd "antennas" of one group of slaves detected trouble for another group. For example, Susan Broaddus worked in the white folks' Big House where she overheard the slave master exclaim: "Gonna sell 'em, I swear fo' Christ, I gonna sell 'em." But Broaddus could not read or write. Knowing of his house servant's illiteracy, the master spelled the name of the two slaves he intended to sell further south into a harder and more cruel life in slavery. Susan Broaddus made "believe I didn't even hear" as the master spoke the letters of the chattel to be sold. But she "was packin' dem letters up in my haid all de time" and the first opportunity she got, she hurried out to the slave quarters and unpacked those letters to her own father "an' say 'em to him jus' like Marsa say 'em." Immediately her father, who could read and spell, notified the two slaves in question. The next day the two "had run away. . . . Dey never could fin' dose two slaves. Was gone to free land!"[63]

Clearly, to get to free land individual slaves relied upon multifarious communal ingenuity and stratagems. However, in the individual-collective definition of African American humanity, the most organized and efficient black political resistance—short of the slaves' victory in the Civil War—was the Underground Railroad with Moses, known more familiarly as Harriet Tubman, leading the way. Harriet Tubman set out for freedom one day by walking off of her white master's plantation in Maryland. Yet God spoke with her in such a way that she believed her own liberated existence, after successfully reaching "up north," contained a void as long as the remainder of her former slave community languished under the whimsical whips of wicked whites "down south." Though she had tasted the fruit of freedom, the plight of her fellow oppressed humankind and the weight of their dilemma under the institution of slavery moved her to return to the land of "Egypt" under God's instruction to set God's people free. Hence, slaves throughout the South recognized the name of Moses, the captain of the Underground Railroad. For instance, former slave Robert Ellett describes the success of Moses in her elusive moving of slaves from bondage to freedom, from deformed life to full humanity, from Satan's domain to God's kingdom. " 'Moses' would come around" and, relates Ellett, "she would run [slaves] away and get them over near the border line . . . the next night on what you call the 'Underground Railroad.' "[64] In sum, slaves employed both individual and collective courage to pursue their God-given free humanity through the resistance of politics against the wickedness of the slave masters.

THE CULTURE OF RESISTANCE

The anthropological resistance of politics went hand-in-hand with African American theological notions of a culture of resistance. Since slaves understood their created being through the lens of liberation, they defined and forged an appropriate black way of life — a culture of resistance — that provided them with an ethic of survival in the grip of white supremacy. Three instances of this cultural ethic, this lifestyle of black human resistance, will suffice: 1) a taking-not-stealing practice; 2) a duality of survival; and 3) a discourse of solidarity.

Taking-Not-Stealing. Slave masters and their paid Christian ministers constantly exhorted slaves against stealing their masters' livestock and, of course, against stealing away to freedom. White theologians preached against such survival activities on the slaves' part as the work of the Anti-Christ. Instead of obeying their earthly owners, African American chattel rebuffed such doctrinal maxims and differentiated between stealing and taking. They defined "stealing" as the illegal removal of a fellow bondservant's private property and taking as the removal of that which they believed the master had wrongfully stolen from the slaves. One former slave sums up the consensus: "Chile, nigger had to steal, an' I know ma mommer didn't tell no lie." What compelled enchained African Americans to disobey one of the cardinal rules of white law and risk certain brutal punishment if not death? The necessity of sheer survival mandated that they had to preserve their lives, that is, their humanity, by removing the basic provisions of life from the master's till. "See ole Mars and Missus give us such little rations," comments Marrinda Jane Singleton, "led her slaves to stealin'." For slaves, authentic religion and a Christian way of life did not mechanically flow from an abstract white prescription of negativities regarding ethical commands. A perspective from below, a perspective of black human survival, identified and affirmed right and wrong in contrast to those white folks who held privilege and power in society and could thus pontificate, legislate, and propagate the moral axioms of an oppressor class. Furthermore, while white people ate well and wrote sermons and theology about how their black human property should do good and not succumb to ethical impurities, African American chattel suffered emaciated bodies. The slaves "didn't get nothing but fat meat and corn bread and molasses. And they got tired of that same old thing," says one ex-slave. Consequently, they had to "illegally" enter the henhouse to get chickens or the smokehouse to get hams or the vegetable patches to procure adequate nourishment. In a word, they had to define and develop a culture of resistance, a way of life to survive slavery's onslaught on their humanity. As one former slave asks: "That ain't stealin', is it?"[65]

Blacks claimed they learned their "stealing" or "taking" from the biggest rogue of all, the white master. Another ex-bondsman offers his theological, anthropological insight:

> All you hear now is 'bout de nigger stealin' from dese here po' white devils. De whole cause of stealin' an' crime is 'cause dey fo'ced the nigger to do hit in dem back days. ... White folks certainly taught niggers to steal. If they had given them enough to eat dey wouldn' have no cause to steal.[66]

This former slave underscores the insidious ethical nature of whites by classifying them with Satan ("po' white devils"). Hence evil human beings, that is, white humanity, utilized coercion against the children of God; this resulted in the latter's devising a new survival ethic. Whites did not give blacks enough to eat; on the contrary, they intentionally starved African Americans, giving their slaves a "cause to steal."

In addition, because slaves were forbidden normal sustenance, they maintained a historical perspective and connection to their native origins that led them to a new ethical interpretation. They did not suffer historical amnesia about how whites emerged as the dominating social class in North America. Rather, they rebelled against white practices due to the blatant hypocrisy of white theological instructions about the ethics of black humanity.

> "Dey allus done tell us it am wrong to lie and steal," explained Josephine Howard of Texas, "but why did de white folks steal my mammy and her mammy? Dey lives clost to some water, somewher over in Africy. ... Dat de sinfulles' stealin' dey is."[67]

White folks did the first stealing, "de sinfulles' stealin' dey is." How could slave masters discourse about the right and wrong of human practices when they had forcefully taken Africans from their motherland and the protective and watchful eyes of their parents? In Africa blacks had lived in their own political kingdoms with indigenous cultural expressions and theological world-views. Having committed a grave anthropological sin — stealing a race of people from their God-given space on earth — white folks, in the slaves' opinion, would forever reap the whirlwind of their own original sin. Specifically, their black property would never submit to white theology as long as African Americans retained their own historical theological consciousness.

The white slave-master class was not unaware of the theological foundation to black differentiation between stealing and taking. Indeed, a white slave mistress unwittingly surmised the biblical basis for the slaves' "robbing our [whites'] store room, meat house, etc." when she commented that slaves "think it right to steal from us, to spoil us, as the Israelites did the Egyptians."[68] Even in their theological anthropology, black folk upheld a scriptural stance. Just as the Israelites struggled in a land of bondage and formulated their own ethical norms as Yahweh's possessions, poor blacks perceived their plight similarly. To take from a white pharaoh, then, resulted naturally from what Yahweh-God required of God's created offspring. To fall short of what the Divinity required would upset the slaves' theological grasp of their original intended purpose to be free. Hence they developed their culture of resistance, which included their taking-not-stealing practice. Sarah Fitzpatrick succinctly summarizes:

> Niggers didn't think dat stealin' wuz so bad in dem times. Fak' is dey didn't call it stealin', dey called it takin'. Dey sa, "I ain't takin' f'om nobody but ma' mistrus an' Marster, an' I'm doin' dat 'cause I'se hongry!"[69]

Duality of Survival. To further preserve their humanity in their culture of survival black chattel engineered a way of life that dichotomized between a conscious false display of the slave self in the company of the white master and an authentic expression of the true African American self in the presence of fellow enslaved blacks. Slaves viewed their dire straits from the marginalized vantage of ill-equipped underdogs waging a religious and theological war against evil earthly powers. To successfully engage a well-fortified enemy and prove victorious in the long run, then, necessitated the shrewdest possible techniques in one's total way of life. Therefore, on a daily basis slaves cultivated an uncanny astuteness to show one carefully sculptured facade to the white folks in order literally to live another day.

For example, generally blacks regurgitated all the theological catechisms taught by white theologians and preachers. Blacks did their jobs in the fields and in the Big House just as white folks instructed them. Likewise, blacks executed a myriad of other orders forced upon them by slave masters and mistresses. However, this acceptance of the institution of slavery was the "slave" face performed to keep the white folks off balance so that black chattel could survive and plan further the next move in a long-range strategy to be free, to assume full humanity. In his autobiography ex-slave Henry Bibb testifies to this necessary duality: "The only weapon of self defense that I could use successfully, was that of deception." Not only did one defend oneself by politically resisting with physical force, one also preserved one's God-given humanity by culturally utilizing an ethic of deception.

But such a culture of resistance does not necessarily indicate African American fear of whites. Rather, it suggests a sober assessment that the enemy of slave humanity was a formidable opponent, one to be taken very seriously. To avoid becoming "uppity" or "obnoxious" to white folks, blacks feigned acceptance of white anthropological normalcy. Former slave Lunsford Lane writes the following in his narrative:

> Ever after I entertained the first idea of being free, I had endeavored so to conduct myself as not to become obnoxious to the white inhabitants, knowing as I did their power, and their hostility to the colored people.[70]

Once attaining knowledge of their original liberated humanity created by the Divinity ("the first idea of being free"), they consciously conducted themselves in such a manner as to keep slave masters off balance in the black-white relationship on the plantation. They gave whites the appearance of complying submissiveness and good-natured cooperation, for the more whites believed they had total control of blacks, the more blacks received breathing space to chart their next secret move of resistance for freedom.

This duality of survival contained an "African American" face in addition to the "slave" face, the former signifying the true humanity of the bondservants. One gained privileged access into this real face in situations controlled by blacks. The "Invisible Institution" represented the premier example. Here African American life or humanity forged its unadulterated self with the attendance of God's Spirit. Here the full process of conversion positioned the slave forever along the path of deliverance. The "Invisible Institution," in a word, exemplified the raw African American human life. Assembled deep in the woods, with only an overturned pot for protection, African Americans found worship space in which to thrive by maintaining morale in situations that seemed hopeless; preserving mental sanity in the face of the irrational white world; holding on to a sense of definiteness in a world where slaves lacked control of their present and future; refueling their energy in a white world full of sorrow in order to face the next day; synthesizing memories of African religious structures and practices with reinterpreted Christian beliefs to build a unique African American theology under slavery; organizing and plotting slave political and cultural resistance; and praising God for the divine intent of liberation against a world where Marsa branded them with hot irons as white people's slaves. It was this African American face that slaves forever withheld from the slave masters. During an American Freedmen's Inquiry Commission interview in 1863, former slave Robert Smalls gives the interviewer a hint of this duality of survival:

Q. Do the masters know anything of the secret life of the colored people?

A. No, sir; one life they show their masters and another life they don't show.[71]

Slaves not only used craftiness to survive, they also employed a discourse of solidarity.

Discourse of Solidarity. Ex-slave Rev. Ishrael Massie informs us about a cave that a runaway built in the woods during slavery time. Despite the fact that all the slaves, including Rev. Massie, "knew whar he [the fugitive] wuz," no one turned him in to his Massa. Massie explains why: "In dem days, ya kno', niggers didn't tell on each other."[72] Indeed, not to tell on each other proved a vital ethical discourse of solidarity and survival for African American humanity. To betray this slave's cave in the southern backwoods was tantamount to desecrating a place where God had revealed the inherent gift of freedom through the inevitable laws of nature. Fellow slaves, then, could not surrender the space in which a co-chattel had liberated himself or herself, responding to the free grace of deliverance offered by Jesus in the wilderness. Moreover, an escaped slave graphically symbolized the efficient success of blacks' politics of resistance and culture of politics. The longer the escapee survived, the more he or she gave fellow sufferers hope for ultimate freedom.

Furthermore, no adherent to a liberating theology, a religious experience constructed out of the poor's biblical interpretation, would fracture the religious individual-collective dynamic ("all us slaves knew whar he wuz"). They all knew of the fugitive's whereabouts. But they were likewise cognizant of their own tradition, which rightly perceived the freedom of the individual as immensely benefiting the potential or realized emancipation of the collective, and vice versa. Also, to break the discourse of solidarity ("didn't tell on each other") would be to submit to white folks' religious and theological instructions—"slaves obey your masters." Similarly, abdication to white theology would confirm blacks' actual allegiance to the kingdom of Satan—the peculiar institution of slavery. Then all that the "Invisible Institution" stood for would amount to nought. To the contrary, those words, "don't tell on each other," articulated bondservants' dogged refusal and life-and-death determination not to commit suicide of the self, that is, not to mimic white theology. A former slave from another plantation echoes the sacred vow: "You see we never tole on each other."[73] Though legally private property belonging to whites, slaves defiantly refused to tell on each other in order to uphold their natural African American humanity. God had created them and, to keep the faith in God's grace, they delved into all possible political and cultural resistance.

CONCLUSION

After successfully defeating the Confederacy in the Civil War, four million African Americans claimed their freedom. We saw how they attributed that historic accomplishment to God sending "de war" and to Jesus the Warrior and Liberator. Between 1619, when the initial group of Africans stolen from their homeland arrived in the "New World," and 1865, the conclusion of the Civil War, black chattel mixed the remnants of their African traditional religions with biblical Christianity. In particular, they illegally and secretly met and worshiped in the "Invisible Institution." Over two hundred years of surreptitious religious gatherings allowed them to create a coherent and dynamic theology, which, if today's African American church is to take itself seriously, cannot be ignored. How can contemporary black ecclesial gatherings continue to drift on and be tossed to and fro by the battering and deleterious waves of white theology without an authentic Christian rudder? How can the black church call itself church if it refuses systematically to study and learn from the profound experience of its slave foreparents with the Divine? Truly, over two hundred years of African American "God-talk" provides an abundant source for the development of a contemporary black theology.

But this chapter has only scratched the surface. We have discovered the beginnings of some of the key elements needed in the constructive task for today's black theology. For instance, we saw how slave theology verified the intimate link between the church and the community, a connection that does not pit the sacred against the secular, as in certain elements in Euro-American theology. Because God rules all of creation, slaves understood that the political and the cultural dimensions of life carried theological implications. Moreover, to segregate religion and leave the secular to the secularist is, in fact, to surrender black humanity to heretical faith assertions perpetrated by the demonic dimensions of white theology. We also discovered the emphasis on the communal nature of the "Invisible Institution."

Drawing on their African traditional religions and the Bible, the Old Testament in particular, slaves could only comprehend total deliverance as including the individual and the community. Thus they did not fall prey to a white capitalist theological precept that glorifies individualism and private-property democracy. Today's black theology has to promote individuality and communalism, not individualism and selfish motivations.

Furthermore, the black theology of the "Invisible Institution" tells us about the importance of perseverance through cross-bearing. For over two centuries African Americans endured and resisted white Christian assaults on black humanity. Through prayer and proper supplication to God, with Jesus as the captain of their old ship of Zion, and through the Spirit's empowerment, black folks made it through to emancipation. Paraphrasing old slave wisdom, "God may not come when you call him, but he's right on time!"

Thus the slaves' religious story verifies a contemporary black theological emphasis on doing theology from the perspective of the black poor. To deny this theological privilege is to betray the African American church's Christian tradition. We only hear God's word of liberation and salvation from the position of God's hearing and freeing a marginalized community as that chosen community moves toward justice. Moreover, since God freely gives deliverance to those who have nothing to lose in this world, black theology today must discern the signs of the times in the political and cultural life of the black church and community. And so, God's self is revealed in attempts to alter unjust power relations and in the linguistics, thought forms, and way of life of the have-nots.

Finally, slave religious experience based itself on the Bible. African Americans under white slavery glued themselves to a theology filled with the "let my people go" witness of Yahweh in the Old Testament and with Jesus the Liberator of the poor in the New Testament. It is this faith, this black theology, that powered them through over two centuries of white theological heresy and white supremacy. Therefore, when their penultimate judgment day arrived, we can appreciate the following account of a former slave regarding the Civil War's end:

[When freedom came] we was dancin' an' prancin' an' yellin' wid a big barn fir jus' ablazin' an' de white folks not darin' to come outside de big house. Guess dey [the slaves] made 'em up [spirituals], 'cause purty soon ev'ybody fo' miles around was singin' freedom songs. One went like dis:

I's free, I's free, I's free at las'!
Thank God A'mighty, I's free at las'![74]

2

THE SLAVE NARRATIVES AS A SOURCE OF BLACK THEOLOGICAL DISCOURSE: THE SPIRIT AND ESCHATOLOGY

GEORGE C. L. CUMMINGS

In all the books that you have studied, you never have studied Negro history, have you? You studied about the Indians and white folks, but what did they tell you about the Negro? If you want Negro history, you will have to get it from somebody who wore the shoe, *and by and by from one to the other, you will get a book.*

(Mr. Reed, former slave)

The challenge of contemporary black theological discourse in the United States is to determine the values, symbols, and images from the black experience that will empower the contemporary black liberation struggle. The challenge to continue to devise a black theology that is distinctively grounded in the historical experience of African American people has been articulated in a variety of contexts.[1] The aim of this essay is to contribute to contemporary black theology in the United States by engaging in the process of utilizing the slave narratives as a source for theological ideas and interpreting the significance of the Spirit and the eschatology in them.

46

As a black Christian theologian of liberation, my approach is defined by an a priori commitment to the struggles for liberation of the black oppressed. On the basis of this commitment I engage the slave narratives with the biblical text in order to establish mutually critical correlations between these sources of theological discourse. The ultimate aim is the discernment of the Spirit of Christ the Liberator, who constitutes the basis of the community's ongoing struggle for liberation, and the empowerment of the black oppressed so that they might better understand themselves, sustain their hope, and continue the struggle to transform their circumstances.

In the next section I will describe and interpret the meaning of the experiences of the Spirit testified to in these slave narratives.

THE SPIRIT IN THE SLAVE NARRATIVES

The testimony of thousands of ex-slaves is based upon their experiences and on the witness of others. The entrance of the Spirit meant that there was something in their lives that made a difference. Sarah Emery Merrill testifies:

Many of the old negroes were ignorant, they could neither read nor write. They knew that the entrance of "the Spirit of God" made a difference in their lives but they did not know how to express it only in their limited way.[2]

The coming of the Spirit meant preeminently that someone was "getting religion" or being converted. Mose Hursey, an ex-slave from Louisiana shares:

I heared them git up with a powerful force of the Spirit, slappin they hands and walkin' round the place. They'd shout "I got the glory. I got that old time 'ligion in my heart." I seen some powerful "figurations" of the Spirit in them days.[3]

Getting religion was manifested in a variety of ways. Some slaves had visions, others shouted and walked, and still others bore witness to the creative power of the Spirit. The Spirit possessed the physical being of the slaves, and as a consequence they shouted, spoke of great visions of God, heaven, or freedom, and engaged in physical activity that manifested the Spirit's presence. Conversion testimonies manifest a spiritual presence or power that often had as a consequence a message or mission. In a series of conversion testimonies compiled in the book *God Struck Me Dead*, these elements are clearly present.[4] Nancy Williams, who had been 12 years old when the Civil War began, gave testimony of her own experience:

> Kin 'member how I got my 'ligion. Won' no preachers roun' jes' hada get de Lawd yo'self. Made up my min' I'se gonna run de overseer off de stump. Twas one day in de fiel Jennie an' me was plowin' side by side wid ole slow ox, plowin in cawn, an' she say to me, "Looky here, when you gonna git 'ligion?" I say, "I ain in no hurry!" Feared I miss de substance an ketch de shadow. I'se been six month scratchin' for his stuff I got here. Wanna be sure. I believe twas dat same day, time come fer me to get dat five minute res' at de en' o' de row. Seem lak when I lef' de plow de Spirit struck me. Den I runned cross de fiel jes' a shoutin'. Jumped over de tall rail fence an' de rails come a-tumblin' on me—all but three. Deed, I'se layin' dere in de weeds dead in sin. I stayed dere; my soul an body shinin' lak a mawnin star! ... Don' know how long I stayed dere, but when I come to, I jump up off'n dat bench an' start a-runnin' an a-shoutin'. Went thew de cawn an' broke down all de cawn. Jumped dem rails, fell on dother side wid a bumb. Thought sure I'se in heaven, I had viewed de way in a vision. Dat day I foun' out ya home in heaven got to come f'om God.[5]

Nancy Williams had gone on a spiritual journey; like Jeremiah, Isaiah, Jacob, and Jonah, she had been empowered by the Spirit to transcend her experience of being a slave working in the field and had been taken to a place where she "viewed *de way* in a *vision*" and discovered that the true home was as a child of God. Assurance and security concerning her identity as a human being, one of those redeemed by God, was guaranteed in her mind by means of an experience of the Spirit in which she travelled home, had a vision, and came to find "de way."

This experience parallels the various experiences of innumerable slaves who were taken over by the power of the Spirit and who "trabelled on" to their home. In discussing this, Mechal Sobel notes that the concept of the spiritual traveler is characteristic of the African religio-cultural world-view and contends that "in traveling to a christian heaven, while yet alive, Afro-Americans made the future into the past, into an event that had already occurred. Thus, they used the African time sense (of present and past) to encompass the christian's messianic sense of time future and to make it real."[6] The Spirit took over, made one aware of one's existence as a child of God and as a sinner, and these events were a powerful affirmation of security and assurance in a world that was subject to the whims and attitudes of racist, brutal overseers and slave masters.

An ex-slave named Cornelius Garner noted:

De preaching us got 'twont' nothing much. Dat ole white preacher jest was tellin us slaves to be good to our masters. We ain't keer'd a bit 'bout dat stuff he was telling us cause we wanted to sing, pray and serve God in our own way. You see, 'ligion needs a little motion—specially if you gwine feel de spirret.[7]

The Spirit's presence, according to Garner, entailed the affirmation of independence and selfhood; sustained hope for freedom as embodied in their prayer life; served as the basis of love within the slave community; and even assisted slaves in their desire to escape to freedom. The Spirit's sustaining power/presence was nurtured in the secret meetings where black slaves disobeyed their masters' orders to serve God, sustained their sense of personal identity and well-being, and provided mutual support for each other by giving meaning and hope to their tragic existence. According to Susan Rhodes:

We used to steal off to de woods and have church, like de Spirit moved us—sing and pray to our own liking and soul

> satisfaction — and we sure did have good meetings, honey — baptise in de river like God said. We had dem spirit-filled meetings at night on de bank of de river and God met us dere.[8]

The slaves' autonomy and independence could be expressed in their defiance of their white masters as they sought to communally provide a supportive context for each other. Their religious independence became a means of defying the dominant powers and creating their own means of coping with the reality of their exploitation and suffering. This defiance, born of the Spirit, was poignantly expressed when the ex-slaves talked about the prayers of the slave community. The testimony of an ex-slave from Alabama, William Moore, is shared by many of the other testimonies:

> Seem like niggers just got to pray; half they life is in prayin'. Some nigger take turn 'bout with nuther nigger to watch to see if Marse Tom anyways 'bout and then they circle themselves 'bout on the floor in the cabins and pray. Then they get to moanin' low and gentle, "someday, someday, someday ... this yoke going to be lifted off'n our shoulders ... someday, someday, someday."[9]

Another slave shared:

> I've heard 'em pray for freedom. I thought it was foolishness, then, but the old-time folks always felt they was to be free. It must have been something 'vealed unto 'em.[10]

While many slaves were not allowed to go to church, or to have their own independent church meetings, they

> w'uld whisper roun' an', all meet, in de woods, an' pray.

According to Barney Alford of Mississippi,

> Sum uf de slaves wud git to gedder at night time an' go down by de crick an' pray for to be sot free.[11]

Ellen Butler supports the view that praying for freedom was an expression of the way in which the Spirit led the slaves to defy their masters. She testified:

Massa never 'lowed us slaves to go to church but they have big holes in the fields they gits down in and prays. They done that way 'cause the white folks didn't want them to pray. They used to pray for freedom.[12]

Praying for freedom was the creative expression of the slaves' belief that God did not want them to be slaves but to be free. Thus the Spirit's presence led them to disobey their masters in order to obey God. As the people of Israel prayed for freedom in the Hebrew Scriptures, and the biblical record testifies that God heard their cry, so too African slaves prayed to God for their freedom (Ex 2:23-24, KJV). Just as the Hebrew midwives disobeyed Pharaoh when he commanded them to kill the male offspring of the Hebrew women, so too black slaves disobeyed their white masters in order that they might be obedient to God. The testimony of the Hebrew midwives resonates with the testimony of black slaves:

But the midwives feared God, and did not as the King of Egypt commanded them, but saved the men children alive (Ex 1:17, KJV).

The Spirit was linked with their creativity in the face of their oppression:

I uster knowed lots of spiritual songs but I can't reckileck dem now. Spiritual songs, dey come through visions. Dats why de cullud folks kin mek dem and sing dem better dan de w'ite folks.[13]

Howard Thurman was one of the scholars who recognized the meaning of the creation of the spirituals in the slave community. Thurman wrote:

The clue to the meaning of the spirituals is to be found in religious experience and spiritual discernment.[14]

This creative power was a means of affirming their personhood, dignity, and rights as human beings made in the creative image of God, and the spiritual was an affirmation of the slaves' right to exist in a society that sought their destruction.

Praying and singing for freedom was an expression of the slaves' hope, which was grounded in their understanding that God was a God of justice and freedom. According to the testimony of Carey Davenport and Anderson Edwards:

Sometimes the cullud folks go down in dugouts and hollows and hol' dey own service. They uster sing songs what come a-gushin up from the heart.[15]

When darkies prayed in slavery they darsn't let the white folks know 'bout it or they beat them to death. When we prayed we turned a wash pot down to the ground to catch the voice. We prayed lots in slavery to be free and the Lord heard our prayer. We didn't have no song books, the Lord gave us our songs. When we sing them at night 'roun the fire place it would be just whispering like so the white fo'ks not hear us. We would hum them as we wo'ked in the fiel'.[16]

John White from Oklahoma gave a testimony that connected slave experiences of the Spirit of the Lord with creative opportunities to escape:

The slaves would pray for to get out of bondage. Some of them say the Lord told them to run away. Get to the North. Cross the Red River. Over there would be folks to guide them to the free states.[17]

Their encounter/visions with the Spirit enabled them to have the courage and hope to translate their experiences of hope into concrete actions of escaping to freedom. To the north was freedom and crossing the river, as did the Israelites crossing the Red Sea, would bring them to freedom. The religious imagination played a powerful role in creating new horizons of possibility that linked experiences of the Spirit with the struggle for earthly freedom. Another slave from Texas named Joe Oliver gave a testimony that resonates with John White's:

> Dey singin' an' shoutin' till de break of day. Some goin' into trances an' some speakin' in what dey called strange tongues, dis wuz a good chance for de slaves to run away, for wen' de would rise up from dey trance some would run like de debbil wuz after him, an jes keep runnin' until he run clear off. So de w'ite folks den puts de trusty niggers to guard de door or de way dey leaves if hit in de arbor, but hit is hard to make de trusty catch dem for dey think hit de Holy Ghost dat is makin' dem run, so dey is afraid to stop dem, claimin' dey can't stop de Holy Ghost.[18]

It is evident from the testimony of a wide variety of ex-slaves that they attributed much of their ability to survive crushing oppression to the power of the Spirit of God. Jane Pyatt from Virginia viewed the Spirit of God as having given her the ability to read and goes on to infer that the force of the Spirit is responsible for the respectful and loving relationship in the slave community. She says:

> Most of the time there was no force back of the respect the slaves had for each other, and yet, they were for the most part truthful, loving and respectful to one another.[19]

Charlie Bowen from Texas concurs with Jane Pyatt on the relationship between getting religion and acquiring an education:

> I 'fessed religion way back in slavery time. The Lord gave me what education I got. I can read the bible and write a little.[20]

The lives of black slaves, according to their testimonies, were filled with the consequences of the presence of the Spirit: secret meetings, which were an expression of independence; disobeying their masters in order to serve God in prayer and worship; getting practical tools to help with confronting life; hope; visions

of freedom; and physical manifestations of being possessed by
the Spirit. In the midst of the dialectic of struggle and hope
black slaves attributed their hope to the Spirit of God. Of those
who survived slavery, no one expressed a sense of self-hood
better than George Cato:

> Yes sah! I sho does come from dat old stock who had de
> misfortune to be slaves, but who decided to be men, at
> one and de same time, and I'se proud of it.[21]

The slaves' accounts of their encounters with the presence of
the power of God in the Spirit and of the significance of these
visions provide us with insight into their courage, hope, and
extraordinary heroism in the face of suffering and oppression.
Their encounters with the Spirit became the basis of their
eschatological hope in the God who would ensure their future.

ESCHATOLOGY IN THE SLAVE NARRATIVES

The eschatological hopes that emerge from these interviews
reflect a connection between the presence of the Spirit of God
and the hopes and aspirations of the slave community. My aim
here is to engage in the descriptive/interpretive task as the slaves
tell their story. As much as eschatology, traditionally, has been
defined as that which constitutes the basis of human hope, then
Carl Braaten correctly asserts:

> The meaningfulness of Christian eschatology depends on
> its structural correspondence to the factor of hope in
> human life. Eschatology promises fulfillment; hope pre-
> supposes something lacking. Human beings hope for what
> they lack. If we are in bondage, we hope for deliverance;
> if we sit in darkness, we hope for light. The lack may be
> described by such metaphors as illness, darkness, slavery,
> alienation, lostness, exile, even death. It is the mission of
> hope to respond to a situation of distress by sending out
> a signal for help.[22]

As noted earlier, the presence of the Spirit was seen by slaves
as the basis for their prayers for freedom "someday," and they

were willing to engage, on the basis of that hope, in acts of defiance against masters who had the power of life and death over them, in order to obey God, affirm their rights as human beings, and in some cases escape from slavery. Anderson Edwards tells of the content of his preaching in the presence of his master, on the one hand, and in his absence, on the other:

> I'se been preaching the gospel and farming since slavery time. I jined the chu'ch eighty-three years ago, when I was a slave of Master Gaud. Till freedom, I had to preach what they told me to. Master made me preach to the other niggers that the good book say that if niggers obey their master, they would go to heaven. I knew there was something better for them, but I darsen't tell them so, 'lest I done it on the sly. That I done lots. I told the niggers — but not so master could hear it — that if they keep praying the Lord would hear their prayers and set them free.[23]

The tension of living amid despair and hope, hopelessness and courage, powerlessness and expectant optimism is immediately evident in his testimony. The clash between optimism and pessimism was resolved in knowing that "there was something better for them," which resulted in the subversive message that if they prayed God would answer their prayers and bring freedom. God had revealed that there was a future of freedom for them that was guaranteed by the presence of the Spirit.

Evidently, Anderson Edwards had an eschatological hope that grounded his preaching and activity in the Spirit. He continued,

> Master had told us that if we be good niggers and obey him that we would go to heaven. But I felt all the time there was something better for me. So I kept praying for it till I felt the change in my heart. I was by myself down by a spring when I found the Lord.[24]

According to Edwards's testimony, his encounter with the Spirit of the Lord and consequent change of heart is primordially linked to his hope for freedom and a transformed future.

Yearning for freedom, praying for freedom, preaching for freedom, and working for freedom were concrete expressions of the eschatological views of the slaves and of their life in the Spirit.

John Crawford, a Mississippi ex-slave, explained that he believed that his mother's prayers were based on a hope that was realized in Abraham Lincoln:

> At night in our little log cabin in the quarters Mammy bring the wash pot out of the yard an set it in the middle of the floor and she laugh and cry and sing a little, then she puts her head down in the pot clear to her shoulders and mumbles. We chilluns say "What you sayin' Mammy?" She say "I'm prayin' for the freedom" ... strangest thing is that while Mammy was in her spell of prayin' that a little boy was eight-year old up North who grew up and set the niggers free.[25]

In addition to the views that linked the promise of freedom and hope for the future with the life of the Spirit, the slaves had special views on the presence of the eschaton and its future fulfillment. In other words, they knew something about heaven and hell, as well as of who would occupy each place. Uncle George King believed that hell was the plantation where he had been born in South Carolina, and that the devils there had been white people. The interviewer explains that Uncle George will

> tell you that he was born on two hundred acres of hell, but the white folks called it Samuel Roll's Plantation ... [with] plenty room for that devil overseer to lay on the lash and plenty room for the old she-devil mistress to whip mammy til' she was just a piece of living raw meat.[26]

For George King hell and devils were a present reality in his concrete historical experience. Another ex-slave spoke of being present at the deathbed of his master and having the master tell them "to bring him seven thousand dollars to pay [his] way out of hell" and commenting that his master "coudn'ta got out of hell, the way he beat my mammy."[27] Jack Maddox expressed similar views during an interview in which he and his wife Rosa shared their experiences:

> Yes, I was born a slave and so was Rosa. We got out of the chattel slavery, an I was better for getting out, but Rosa don't think so. . . . She say her white folks were good to her. But don't you expect me to love my white folks. I love them like a dog loves hickory. I was settin' here thinking the other night 'bout the talk of them kind of white folks going to heaven. Lord God, they'd turn the heaven wrong side out and have the angels working to make something they could take away from them. I can say these things now. I'd say them anywhere—in the courthouse, before the judges, before God. 'Cause they done done all to me that they can do.[28]

Heaven was viewed as a place of eternal rest where "someday . . . we'll be free of the yoke of bondage." Their hope was to be free. Slave testimony viewed death, heaven, and escape as possibilities for alleviating their great burden of bondage; their persistent hope for the future was tied to their faith in God. What would the future be like for black oppressed slaves?

Perhaps the word *reversal* is the best description. Heaven was to be a reversal of the present order. In the present they had no home, but in heaven they did. "My Lord! Po' mourner's got a home at las'. Mourner's got a home at las'." In the present they were enslaved, but in heaven freedom awaited. "And before I'll be a slave, I'll be buried in my grave, and go home to my Lord and be free." Moreover, the easy freedom of the white slave holder would be reversed. Frederick Douglass claims "slaves knew enough of the orthodox theology of the time to consign all bad slave holders to hell."[29] That is, the future eschaton meant judgment by a just God: "You shall reap what you sow."

The future meant mercy for slaves and retribution for their masters. In fact, sometimes they were very specific about the reversal of the present order of exploitation, saying that in the life to come there would be black and white people, but the white people would be slaves and the black people would have dominion over them. However, the most basic and commonly expressed aspect of the reversal in the narratives and conversion stories is that God will turn death into life, a life of freedom and justice.

It is this future reversal that aroused discontent and made the present subject to radical change. The exciting vision of what was to come released the power of the future into their lives, bringing not only the strength to survive but also the courage to strive toward freedom. The eschaton was not an opiate; it functioned proleptically. The transcendent future was also the present. The "home over yonder" and the "promised land" of the spirituals were for the slaves both an "otherworldly" promise and a "this worldly" hope for freedom.

In fact, when the slaves sang words like "O Canaan, sweet Canaan, I am bound for the land of Canaan," it is often hard to distinguish whether they meant life after death or a freed life in the North or back in Africa. One simply has to conclude that both meanings were intended, that they anticipated the future in the present, and that the future was occurring ahead of time, that is, proleptically. This is beautifully expressed in the words of Harriet Tubman when she gained her freedom in the North. "I looked at my hands to see if I was de same person now I was free. Dere was such a glory ober de fields, and I felt like I was in heaven."[30]

That the transforming power of the final future was experienced proleptically by the slaves is most evident in the slave conversion stories from the book *God Struck Me Dead*. The experience of being "struck dead" was a proleptic experience. With "death" came the end and the future reversal. In the conversion stories it is as if the Spirit transports them from their present strife to the end and they see, hear, and feel God's act of deliverance. For example, in the story "Waist-Deep in Death," we find this passage:

> Then God took me off. I experienced death, the way I'm going to die. . . . I heard groaning while in hell. Then he lead me into the greener pastures.[31]

The experience of being led through a judgment scene and then arriving in heaven is common. The passage from the conversion story "God Struck Me Dead" is perhaps the most telling:

The Father, the Son, and the Holy Ghost led me on to glory. I saw God sitting in a big armchair. I saw the lamb's book of life and my name written on it. A voice spoke to me and said, "Whosoever my son sets free is free indeed. I give you a through ticket from hell to heaven. Go into yonder world and be not afraid, neither be dismayed, for you are an elect child and ready for the fold."[32]

The future salvation and liberation of the person is truly experienced. The freedom of the end becomes real in the present. And with this proleptic experience of heaven comes the call to go back unafraid into "yonder world," the world of oppression. The experience of heaven, that one is an elect child and free, gives strength to continue in the struggle. The call to go back to do God's will, after the conversion experience, is also common in the stories.[33] Therefore, the conversion experience was inseparable from the present.

THE SPIRIT AND ESCHATOLOGY IN THE SLAVE NARRATIVES

Black theology asserts the priority of the black experience of enslavement and a struggle for liberation as the starting point of black theological discourse. Close scrutiny of the slave narratives shows that they can provide the raw material for an interpretation of the Spirit and eschatology in the slave narratives. The slave testimonies to the Spirit and eschatology entail a complex web of counter-hegemonic religio-cultural traditions that constituted the basis of their hope for a transformed future.[34] In addition, the slave narratives testify to the persistence of hope, human dignity, and self-affirmation that bear witness to the presence of the Spirit of God. This was the *pneumatos* (God's Spirit), a liberating presence which created and sustained the will of an enslaved people against those people and institutions that perpetrated the exploitation of African American chattel. Whereas hegemonic religion and culture defined them as less than human, counter-hegemonic traditions functioned as an oppositional force, affirming their humanity and sustaining their hope. There are several dimensions of the Spirit's presence in the slave community that are evident in the testimonies.

The spirit of the Lord was revealed in the radical affirmation of slave autonomy and independence manifest in the slaves' willingness to defy their oppressors in order to serve God. Religious life became a context for the affirmation of one's humanity by praying for freedom, shouting and dancing, holding secret meetings, and disobeying the oppressor. In the context of worship the black oppressed, who had no autonomy during the rest of their weekly routines, expressed themselves physically by dancing and running or orally by shouting. In this communal context black slaves discovered the sense of human self-worth that led them to reject the white oppressors' definition of them. The Spirit of the Lord allowed black slaves to transcend the horizon of their immediate experiences and to hope for a future in which they would be free. Freedom was not an abstract concept but a concrete hope that led them to hope and work for historical freedom. The significance of their expectations of hope and justice are to be found in the promissory character of God's eschatological presence in their community.

Some black slaves who had encountered the Spirit became entranced, danced, shouted, and then ran "clear off," and never returned. The Spirit of God sustained their aspirations as they prayed "someday, someday . . . this yoke will be lifted," and the Spirit was reflected in their ability to confront creatively their circumstances by creating new instruments of survival and liberation. They created the spirituals, one slave commented, because they had been revealed to them.[35] In addition, the Spirit nurtured respect and love in the oppressed community. This highlights the importance of the communal aspect of God's Spirit as it was evidenced in the manner and quality of human relationships within the slave community. The spirit of justice emerged in the slave testimonies as they bear witness to their own judgments concerning justice, righteousness, and good. Masters and mistresses who whipped human beings until they were raw flesh were devils who would go to hell, and they wouldn't be able to buy their way out of it. The witness of the narratives is to the Spirit of the Lord as the one who provided them with the faith to dance. The Spirit was the living and dynamic presence of God the Liberator erupting through the culture, religion, and history of the black oppressed in their struggle for freedom.

Concomitantly, the eschatological hopes and aspirations of the slave community became evident in the Spirit who guarantees the future as one of freedom and justice. The transfiguring presence of the Spirit of the Lord validated the will to freedom found in their testimonies. There is an immanent character to the slave testimonies concerning their visions of freedom. The eschatological views linked their ardent expectations of God's future with their historical struggle for freedom. Faith and hope, expressed in the radical affirmation of autonomy and independence in the slave community, express the ultimate vision of God's future of freedom. Within the meaning-world of the black slave there was an affirmation of the intersection of transcendence and immanence, such that the Holy Ghost could make black slaves escape to freedom. Their heavenly expectations profoundly shaped their earthly aspirations and activities. John White witnesses that the slaves "say the Lord told them to run away, get to the North."[36]

The eschatological expectations shared in the slave testimonies showed that their encounter with the Spirit of the Lord enabled them to evolve a critique of racism and racists, dream a grand vision of freedom, nurture communal relationships, fight for freedom, defend each other, affirm their humanity, and hear the melody of the future with such clarity that they literally, in faith, were prepared at great cost to dance to the melody of the future by acting in the present to create it. "Strangest thing," said ex-slave John Crawford, "is that while Mammy was in her spell of prayin' that a little boy was eight-year old up North who grew up and set the niggers free."[37]

IMPLICATIONS FOR A CONTEMPORARY BLACK THEOLOGY (USA)

From the perspective of contemporary black theology in the United States, the heart of Christian expectation and hope is that the oppressed One of God—the resurrected One—whose presence is celebrated in the community of faith, is the one who is witnessed to in the slave narratives as the Spirit of the Lord.

The hermeneutical basis for linking Jesus of Nazareth, and his message concerning the reign of God, with the manifestation of God as Liberator in black history and black culture, is pneumatology. This is the methodological ground whereby the black theologian in the United States is able to assert that the Christ is black. The theological appropriation of a doctrine of the Spirit as the creative, empowering, hope-inducing power in the black experience explains how it is that a prophet of ancient Palestine, Jesus of Nazareth, can be viewed as being continuously accessible throughout human history.

The importance of this insight lies in the assertion that the Spirit of Christ provides a hermeneutical key by which to establish continuity between Jesus of Nazareth and the liberating presence of Christ as the Black Messiah. Jesus of Nazareth, according to the testimony of the early church, was the embodiment of God in the world (Col 2:9). God is the story of Jesus, and the story of Jesus of Nazareth as the Crucified One is an expression of God's heart for these who are being crucified by enslavement and oppression. Accordingly, then, the Spirit of Christ is the theological link between Jesus of Nazareth, the Galilean Jew, and the Christ of faith present in the experiences of black enslaved people who joined Jesus in his cry on the cross, "My God, my God, why hast thou forsaken me?" (Matt 27:46).

There are five aspects of the biblical tradition and the church's belief in the Holy Spirit that are relevant here: 1) the Spirit of God as the gracious gift of God; 2)the Spirit as a means of preventing us from objectifying God; 3) the Spirit as the Spirit of Christ; 4) the Spirit as stressing the eschatological character of God; and 5) the Spirit as the Spirit of mission. First, the Holy Spirit is understood in the biblical tradition as a gracious gift from God (Eph 2:8) that liberates us from all that restricts and restrains human potentiality. The testimony and experiences of black ex-slaves witness to the miraculous and gracious gift of God's Spirit in their midst.

Second, the doctrine of the Spirit in the biblical tradition helps to prevent the objectification of God (Jn 3:8). Paul's testimony to the Athenians at the Areopagus is that faith in Christ entails the belief in a God that cannot be reduced to temples or objects of human worship (Acts 17:16-31). Paul's stress is upon the God of life as a creative presence within the same reality shared by humanity (v. 24); the trust entailed by Christian faith in a living God "in whom we live and move and have our being" (v. 28); and the fact that finding God is a matter of reaching out and discerning God's presence, for God "is not far from each one of us" (v. 27). The story of Cornelius and Peter, the God-Fearer (Acts 10), reminds us that the Spirit of God cannot be limited to the community of faith or its ritual acts and places, since God's Spirit is accessible, even to outsiders. This concept of the Holy Spirit can assist us in resisting the temptation to objectify God as a means of control and manipulation.

Third, the Christian tradition stresses that the Spirit is the Spirit of Christ (Lk 1:35; Rom 1:4; Jn 16:13-15). Herein lies James Cone's insistence on the distinctively Christian character of Black Theology in the United States of America (BTUSA).[38] The Black Messiah is the dynamic presence of the Spirit of Christ empowering the poor to struggle for liberation. The Christian perspective is grounded distinctively in our memory of Jesus of Nazareth, who was called the Messiah and whose presence must continually be discerned in the struggles of the poor.

Fourth, the biblical concept of the Spirit stresses the eschatological character of the reality of God as a presence that points to a new and transformed future (2 Cor 5:1-5; Eph 1:11-15). The presence of the Spirit as a means of discovering new horizons of faith and hope has a promissory dimension.

Fifth, the Spirit in the Bible points to a commitment in mission to the poor (Lk 4:16-19). The Spirit calls forth and motivates faith and hope in struggle. In sum, the Spirit of Christ is God's gift to the poor; it empowers and motivates them in the struggle; it resists the temptation of reducing God's Spirit to the historical struggle; it encourages them to look for God in all creation; and it motivates the mission of religio-cultural, socioeconomic, and political liberation among them.

So defined, the Spirit as the Spirit of Christ, understood as the embodiment of the values and commitments manifested in the life, ministry, and message of Jesus of Nazareth and as the gift of the liberating presence of the Messiah among the poor, provides us with the basis for interpreting the Spirit in the slave narratives as the Spirit of Christ. It is this Spirit that caused Mollie Dawson to testify:

De slaves was about de same things as mules or cattle. Dey was bought and sold, and dey wasn't supposed ter be treated lak people, anyway. *We all knew dat we was only a race of people, as our maser was*, and dat we had certain rights, but we was jest property and had ter be loyal ter our masters. It hurts us sometimes ter be treated de way some of us was treated, but we couldn't help ourselves and had ter do de best we could, which nearly all of us done.[39]

For the early Christian community, God's kingdom was Christ's kingdom manifested in the presence of the Spirit as they (the community of Jesus) incarnated the values that Jesus promulgated. They struggled to create the kingdom; at the same time they recognized that the coming kingdom stands *extra nos* (beyond us). Hence my view of pneumatology is one that views the Spirit of Christ as extending beyond Jesus of Nazareth, the church, and the oppressed to a God whose resurrection is the concrete basis of the hope of the poor and the oppressed for a new and different future. The Spirit of Christ is a living presence that points beyond the limitations of each historical situation and is the ongoing basis for the community's will and struggle from brokenness and exploitation toward wholeness and *shalom*.

There are several insights that are relevant for the continued development of a contemporary black theology of liberation in the United States of America. First, the dialectic of despair and hope as a constitutive part of existence becomes the basis for the identification of oppressed people with a God who experiences crucifixion. There is no need to rationalize the existence of evil within the African American slave experience. In fact, the genius of the religion of the black slave was that they transformed Christianity and utilized it to raise their experience to a higher level of meaning. Black slaves, through the use of the traditional religions and Christianity, transformed these brute encounters with raw and meaningless suffering into an experience of hope. By an identification with Jesus Christ and participation in his paradigmatic experience of crucifixion, which included both tragedy and hope, black slaves came to view God's presence in the Spirit as an empowering presence that provided them with the means to confront the reality of their absurd experience. By affirming heaven as their home and the plantation as hell, they resisted white racist attacks on their collective humanity and provided a subversive indictment of the prevailing reality of white racism.

Second, black slaves' insistence that the connection between their religious experiences and the struggles of this world was, and is, a reaffirmation of the traditional African concept of the wholeness and integration of life. Religion was a dimension of life that pervaded every aspect of the slave community's life. Their "sacred" world was linked with the "profane" world. The sacred was the essence of all dimensions of life. In addition, black slaves acknowledged the connectedness among the past, present, and future and gave testimony to the manner in which the future of God became present to them and enabled them to continue in hope. A contemporary black theology should affirm a unitary view of life and of history, and reject the dualisms that are characteristic of traditional theology. Theology and politics are insolubly connected with each other. The kingdom of God's future manifests itself in this world in concrete historical communities where crucified people discover hope.

Third, the slave narratives testify to a world-view that affirmed the shared character of communal life where the Spirit is shared as the Spirit of courage, hope, grace, and victory. Herein lies the significance of the community's shared experience of worshiping God, praying together for freedom, and being joined in the Spirit. The common black experience of tragic suffering lived in and through the dialectic of hope and resignation is set on a powerful journey in the context of worship, where a qualitative shift in the community's consciousness takes place and serves to liberate momentarily and keep alive the hope of permanent liberation. The communal nature of life and the shared experiences of the Spirit ought to lead black theology to affirm the relational character of the Spirit of Christ. It is in historical human relationships that the power of the Spirit is manifested concretely.

Fourth, the persistent belief of black slaves that justice and freedom would be vindicated by God ought to be central to a contemporary black theology that seeks to empower African Americans to continue to struggle for liberation. Freedom is God's freedom and is manifested in the persistent will of the oppressed to fight and kick against injustice and hopelessness. Jesus Christ is the crucified embodiment of God, who brings about black liberation by joining the black oppressed and sharing with them the resurrecting power of the Spirit.

3

"COMING THROUGH 'LIGION": METAPHOR IN NON-CHRISTIAN AND CHRISTIAN EXPERIENCES WITH THE SPIRIT(S) IN AFRICAN AMERICAN SLAVE NARRATIVES

WILL COLEMAN

I 'member when Moma Hanna come through 'ligion. She was in the house and I heard hur in ther' cryin' and talkin' 'bout her foot been taken out the miry clay and placed on the rock of eternal life . . . wind may blow, storm may rise, nothin' a fight hur . . . I went runnin' in ther' crying, "Moma Hanna, Moma Hanna, what ail you? What tha' matter wih you?" She kep' on talkin'. I didn't know nothin' 'bout no 'ligion.

(Alice Coleman)[1]

The above are the words of an 83-year-old matriarch with 149 descendants. On another occasion, she shared the following: "When Moma Hanna died . . . one night I was sleepin'. Moma Hanna keppa mashin' me. She rode me all night. . . . She was gon' worry me ta death." Taken together, these quotations represent a contemporary example of the primary concern of this chapter: how African American people use metaphors to describe both non-Christian and Christian experiences with the spirits and the Spirit as an expression of their own unique form of linguistic-poetic discourse. Some hermeneutical implications of this thesis will be explained as we proceed.

Testifying or telling the story of one's encounter with God is an important aspect of the African American religious experience. Especially within the context of worship in the African American church, it provides an opportunity for members of the community of faith to articulate common beliefs regarding their spiritual reality. The historical antecedents to the institutional African American church were traditional African religions and what came to be known as the "Invisible Institution."[2] The latter was not so much an organization as it was an organic syncretism that enabled slaves to combine their Afrocentric religious beliefs with the Eurocentric ones of their masters. The consequence of this merger was their own unique form of African American Christianity. In many slave narratives that describe "conversion experiences," this process was spoken of metaphorically as "coming through 'ligion." It usually signified a dramatic experience through which slaves understood themselves to have become Christians.

In this essay I will investigate both experiences of the spirits and the Spirit among African American slaves as recounted through selected narratives. It is primarily a hermeneutical consideration of the ways in which slaves experienced the reality of God, their deceased ancestors, and other spiritual beings known in various ways as ghosts, hants, and spirits. I am especially concerned with the borderline or transitional phase (that of "coming through 'ligion") between a traditional African experience of the spirits (through dreams, visions, and other spiritual phenomena) within the North American context, and a more Christian encounter with the Spirit.

In order to interpret the slaves' experiences with the spirits and the Spirit, I will utilize hermeneutical insights from the writings of Paul Ricoeur, especially with reference to 1) the task of hermeneutics; 2) the importance of symbolic and metaphorical language; 3) the function of the narrative genre; and 4) the appropriation of what the text presents.[3] Following a descriptive interpretation of selected texts, I will expand upon some hermeneutical implications related to the above insights and conclude with suggestions concerning the relevance of both non-Christian and Christian African American slave narratives for a black theology of liberation. Since this paper is primarily concerned with the hermeneutical implications of African American slave narratives, a fuller treatment of specific theological themes will be the task of a future project.

Meanwhile, I am convinced that African American slave narratives are a viable source for a contemporary black theology of liberation. Furthermore, I believe that both non-Christian and Christian testimonies provide radical insights into the total religious life of African American slaves. The symbols and metaphors slaves used to express their reality provide the primary articulation of linguistic liberation from both the religious and theological language of their masters. More specifically, I maintain that the slaves' metaphors pressed against the limits of traditional Christian theological conceptualizations. This provides contemporary African American theologians with an opportunity to explore new possibilities for black theology via metaphors taken from both non-Christian and Christian sources. To this end black theology will be strengthened by drinking from the deep fountain of the total African American religious experience, which has been and remains pluralistic. The narratives used in this chapter seek to demonstrate this point.

At the same time, I am aware that in some cases it may be difficult to delineate the "theology" of the African American slaves, since traditional, Eurocentric, Christian theology is by definition critical reflection upon the God who is revealed in the scriptures, especially through the incarnation of Jesus Christ and the work of the Holy Spirit. It may be even more of a misnomer to speak of "doctrines" within certain religious slave narratives, especially those that are not explicitly Christian. Such narratives should be taken as they are recorded without any attempt to Christianize them or make them comply with our presuppositions of what they ought to be saying. They should be allowed to speak for themselves, from the reality found in the text.[4] Consequently, their use as sources for a contemporary black theology will be informed by having heard their testimonies in ways that contribute new insights into the language of liberation.[5] Then we will be in a much better position to consider their theological implications, especially with respect to the symbolic and metaphorical use of language.

The above considerations are crucial when considering a radical notion such as the experience of the spirits in the slaves' religious reality. Under traditional biblical, theological, and psychological categories the former would be designated as either angelic or demonic forces, as something to be demythologized, or as psychotic eruptions.

However, if we really hear the slaves' voices, their experiences of the spirits and the Spirit are available for us to appropriate from a proposed world. This world is discovered in the text. It is a world that we seek to enter into, come to understand, and ultimately make our own. Let us begin by considering testimonies about spirits and the Spirit from representative African American slave narratives.[6]

PHYLLIS GREEN: "DEM AS COULD FLY FLEW HOME"

Phyllis Green, when asked by her mistress if she did not think the slaves were better off in this country where they were taught religion and better ways of living, replied: "I aint know, cause dem as could fly flew home. Dat same ting happen down at Sol Legare fore rebble time."

Phyllis was referring to a legend of Solomon Legare Island (part of James Island). An extensive slave owner had brought back over a new batch of blacks direct from Africa. According to the custom of the time this group was given two weeks in which to adjust themselves to their new surroundings before they were set to work. But in the opinion of Phyllis, supported by the legend itself, these were not ordinary beings. "When dey left by dey self you could hear a tapping, tapping, tapping all day and all night. And dey would not crack dey teet to dem" (would not speak to anyone).

Finally, the time came for the slave driver to call them to work with the crack of his whip. "Dey come out and dey stretch out dey han jest like dey gwine to tek de tools

to wuk like de rest. But when dey stretch dey han dey rise.
At middle day you could see dem far out ober de ocean.
At sundown you could hear 'o voice, but dey couldn't shum
no mo'. Dem gone home."[7]

Phyllis Green of Charleston, South Carolina, is a former
slave. She remembers well how her former mistress, evidently a
Christian herself, looked to her for an affirmation of the positive
influence of Christianity upon people of African descent. This,
however, is precisely what Phyllis refused to give her. In the
mind of Phyllis, there is a legend that summarizes the ambivalence some African American slaves felt toward both the religion and lifestyle of their masters. It is an account of extraordinary human beings who evidently possessed tremendous
powers, which set them apart from the ordinary slave. According
to this legend, they came directly from Africa; they were not
second- or third-generation African Americans. The legend also
implies that they brought their religion and way of life with them
and would not allow their own belief system to be modified by
their new surroundings. In other words, they did not "adjust."
On the contrary, they kept to themselves while plotting a return
to their own country. Finally, "with the crack of the whip," when
it was time for them to demonstrate their willingness to participate in the system that had enslaved them, they pretended to
accommodate the slave driver. But instead, they transformed
themselves into air-borne beings and flew home to freedom. By
noon they still could be seen flying over the Atlantic Ocean. By
sunset, only their voices could be heard. "Dem gone home."

In traditional African religions the nearest counterpart to
these extraordinary human beings would be the spirits of the
air.[8] In this particular legend would-be slaves are transformed
into beings who could not be bound through slavery, Christianity, or Euro-American values. Their memory of Africa
remained too intact for them to "adjust themselves to their new
surroundings."

For Phyllis, this legend expresses both an ambivalence toward
Christianity and a yearning to return to Africa. It also represents
a belief in beings who could transcend the limitations that were

imposed upon ordinary African Americans through slavery, another religion, and an alien culture.

These beings represent spirits that returned to Africa. They symbolize the yearning for liberation from bondage. Through them, many slaves were reminded where their true home was. Furthermore, the myth itself expresses their desire to find their own place in the world separate from the one defined for them by their masters.

AMOS LONG: "MIS' MARTHY'S A-COMIN BACK"

But African American slaves encountered other beings, who either refused to leave the realm of ordinary human beings or returned from the dead. They were called ghosts, spirits, and hants (haints). Some were deceased members of one's family, friends or neighbors. Others were strangers. In the narratives that follow we shall consider the roles of these diverse encounters as they are described in the slaves' own metaphorical language.

"I been settin' up yonder at Mis' Marthy's dis mornin' a-thinkin' 'bout how it use to be when dey was livin' and de great house was full o' life. But Mis' Marthy's a-comin back if dem boys don't carry out her will right. She said de land was to go from heir to heir, and dey done sold it out'n de family. Mis' Marthy'll be back bye 'n' bye, and den — Has I ever seen a goat? Many a one."

"A ghost, Pa," Minnie prompts, laughing.

"Ha'nt, you mean! Yes, mistis, dey's ha'nts. Dey use to hear 'em up yonder at Mis' Marthy's. One night dey was all a-eaten' supper when dey heard somebody walk in de front. Dey sent me to see who was at de do.' Dey wa'n't nobody dere, hadn't been dere. Dat was a common thing — to hear somebody walkin' up de front steps, in de hall, and dey wouldn't be nobody dere.

"Dey'll be some mo' walkin' too. De land was to go from heir to heir. Mis' Marthy wanted de land to stay in de family. Now all dis disputin' over lines and timber 'mongst de chil'en is 'cause dey sold de land. I heard Mis' Marthy say to Mr. Dick 'fore she died: 'Baby, de land is plenty to make a livin' on. De family won't suffer long as dey hold some land. I want mine left so it will go from heir to heir.' "[9]

In Seaboard, South Carolina, Amos is pondering the continuity between life and death. Mis' Marthy, though she is dead, lives. Moreover, in his way of thinking she will make her presence felt from beyond the grave. Disobedience on the part of her heirs will be the catalyst for bringing her spirit back into their world. During her lifetime she had come to realize the importance of owning land and before dying had instructed her sons to pass it on from heir to heir. This would have ensured their right to work their own land instead of toil for someone else. It also would have guaranteed them some protection against dissension within the family, poverty, and homelessness. She had reminded them that "de land is plenty to make a livin' on. De family won't suffer long as dey hold some land." Since they did not honor her will, now they were suffering.

But for Amos, there is an even greater threat: "Mis' Marthy's a-comin back." Like an African ancestress who is displeased by the lack of veneration or respect received from her heirs, she is going to return.[10] In the words of Amos, "Dey'll be some mo' walkin." The spirit of Mis' Marthy symbolizes the interconnectedness between those who are alive and those who have recently died. Moreover, she represents a mutual responsibility that the living and the dead have toward each other. Before dying Mis' Marthy had made provisions for the well-being of her heirs. In return, they were obliged to honor her wishes. According to Amos, the consequence of their failure to do so was both material loss and a haunting psychological punishment.

Mis' Marthy's home is a haven for "ha'nts," who often appear among the living. On the whole, they are either harmless or simply annoying. But under the circumstances of this breach of trust, Amos believes that Mis' Marthy will return with a vengeance. This testimony illustrates both the power of imagination and of memory. On the one hand, Amos holds an image of the consequences of Mis' Marthy's heirs' disregard for her wishes. On the other hand, he underscores the importance of remembering one's heritage, of learning from one's ancestors.

OPHELIA JEMISON: "BAD SPERRITS," OMENS, AND DEATH

In addition to deceased relatives, slaves also described spirits who were either wicked or malevolent. Some were the haunting presence of wicked individuals who had died and returned to torment the wicked who were still alive. Others could find no peace beyond death. These roamed from place to place among the living.

Inteviewer: "Ophelia will you tell me why spirits come back to worry people?"

"Bad sperrits come from hell to torment wicked people what dey 'sociate wid when dey on dis ert [earth]. Sometime dey kill 'em scare. Hell one turrible place. What de wicked do on dis ert, it jes lak dat in hell. Cussing, shooting, fighting one anodder, but dey being sperrits caint do any hurt. De fire down here is a big pit ob brimstone, a roaring an' a roaring. It bigger dan Charleston seem lak. When I was seeking de Lord befo' I conberted [converted] 'e place me in hell to conbince [convince] me. I stay down dere mos' a hour, den I knowed dere a hell. . . .

"When you dream 'bout em dat dead dey sperrit been 'bide wid you when you is sleep. 'E been wanna [want to] tell you somet'ing mos lak, so jes' set youself in mind for somet'ing dat aint go he'p you wedder de storm. One time I dream my mother what been dead long time, was set right dere in de do [door], an' she say, 'Ophelia, is you happy?' den she walk out an' gone. I steady 'bout dat dream all next day, an' I say, 'somet'ing gwine happen,' an' befo anudder day come, deat [death] meet me in dat same do. Me husband brung home, knock down dead, widout one las' word. I griebe ober dat, but de Lord mobe in a mysterious way an' what 'E do is we Christian duty to oncept. A dream dat rest heaby on you mind is a wisitation ob de sperrit. Look on it wid concern."[11]

First of all, it should be noted that Ophelia's response already has been shaded by the interviewer's question: "Will you tell me why spirits come back to worry people?" The interviewer assumes that all spirits are evil. But this is not true. Thus Ophelia corrects this misconception with a description of the role of "bad sperrits" in relation to the living. They are dead people who return from hell to torment wicked people with whom they associated while alive. Sometimes they even frighten them to death. Since both are wicked, their destinies are interwoven. Moreover, their worlds are parallel realities; the spirits of the wicked continue to behave as they had while they were physically alive: "cussing, shooting, fighting one anodder."

However, it also should be noted that Ophelia's vision of hell, one that caused her to become a Christian, is not limited to an agonizing place of torment. Actually, the biblical imagery of eternal damnation has been so altered in her mind that these wicked spirits cannot hurt each other. Nevertheless, she is convinced by her hour-long visitation in hell that she should become a Christian. In many slave narratives dreams, visions, and visitations from spirits are recurrent phenomena that are related to conversion experiences, that is, to becoming a Christian. Therefore, Ophelia's description of this relationship is typical. In addition to conversion experiences, spirits are also associated with signs and omens.

Ophelia believes that spirits of the dead are harbingers of ominous events and possibly death. In fact, it is her mother who comes to haunt her in a dream. Soon afterward, her husband dies. Her interpretation incorporates elements from both folk belief and Christianity.[12] In her mind they are complementary, not contradictory. On the one hand, the Lord works in mysterious ways through dreams and spirits of the dead. On the other hand, "a dream dat rest heaby on you mind is a wisitation ob de sperrit," which may or may not have Christian connotations. In either case, such dreams should be pondered carefully.

Ophelia's beliefs regarding life after death are a reflection of the Christian notion of punishment for deeds committed prior to dying. But this is not necessarily a direct act of God. Neither is it performed by strange supernatural beings as was believed in medieval demonology. Rather, it is retribution received from one's own former associates, one's friends. And further, there is no abrupt change of events between life and death. Instead, the wicked continue to behave exactly as before, repeating familiar patterns. As with the previous narrative, this testimony reflects a belief in the continuity between life and death. Ophelia maintains this conviction even as a Christian.

Also like Amos, Ophelia believes in visitations from one's relatives. Whether her mother comes from heaven or hell to haunt her is unclear. However, her husband's death is considered to be a work of the Lord. Therefore, there seems to be some relationship between the ominous visitation from her mother, her husband's death, and the "mysterious way" of the Lord. Furthermore, all of this is understood within a Christian context. And yet, her reinterpretation of some Christian motifs is an example of reshaping traditional metaphors to suit her own existential situation. She does not restrict them to conventional images of hell, the afterlife, and the spirits. Furthermore, she draws freely from her own experiences, incorporating them into a Christian context.

While for Ophelia belief in spirits represents a somewhat Christian interpretation of their role among the living, the following illustrations are more syncretic in character. These testimonies shared by three Georgians, Mrs. Byrd, Henry Mobley, and Ellen Lindsey, illustrate the syncretic tendency of slaves to combine their Afrocentric beliefs in root medicine, conjure, and spirits with Christianity.

MRS. BYRD, HENRY MOBLEY, AND ELLEN LINDSEY: REMEDIES, APPARITIONS, SPIRITS, AND CONJURE

The following is a home remedy for rheumatism.

"My father wuz sick with rheumatism; and he use ter go through the field with a stick and kill a buzzard, then he would dry him and make gease ter rub his rheumatism with. That wuz a good remedy too, yes sir. Well chile that's 'bout all I know cause I nebber did pay 'tention ter conjure and ghostes."

The following is a story told to Mr. Mobley concerning an apparition.

"I heard once there wuz a women by the name 'uv Carrie Jones. Now this here 'oman wuz wicked and she had a baby that she wuz jest crazy about. Now her baby got real sick and she prayed ter the Lord not ter let her baby die. Once while she wuz praying a light reflected on the wall and Jesus appeared and sed ter her 'You ought ter love me lak you love your baby.' After that, that baby got well and that 'oman got converted and joined the church."[13]

Mrs. Byrd begins by sharing a remedy for rheumatism, while at the same time denying any further knowledge of conjure and ghosts. This is followed by Mr. Mobley's account of Carrie Jones's encounter with the spirit of Jesus in response to a request for the healing of her baby. This, in turn, leads to her conversion and membership in the church. The narrative continues as Mr. Mobley shares his own beliefs in spirits:

I nebber believed in ghosts but I do believe in spirits. Ebby body got two spirits and one is the evil spirit and the other your good spirit. All the time these spirits are wandering about. Do you ebber be sleep and hear somebody call you and it seems lak you can't answer right then? Well thats cause your spirit is away from your body and you can't answer until it returns. Have you ebber dreamed you wuz off visiting in a city you nebber had been in? Well thats your spirit gone there while you wuz sleep. Without the presence of the spirit the body is useless. If a person dies and go ter heaven their spirit is at peace. If a person wuz wicked then their spirit will wander here and there never at peace. [14]

Mr. Mobley describes three different types of relationships with spirits. First of all, he does not believe in ghosts, but in spirits. Since he does not comment on the difference, we can only assume that spirits are more congruous with his experience of reality. Ghosts tend to be associated with the haunting presence of those who died a long time ago and usually are strangers. Spirits refer to those who died more recently and usually are familiar to the person visited by them. Second, with respect to one's own personality, Mr. Mobley holds a peculiar belief that everyone has both an evil and a good spirit.[15] Without saying which spirit does what in dream states, he asserts that it may leave the body at will. Moreover, since the spirit animates the body, the latter is useless without it. And finally, like Ophelia in the previous narrative, he also believes that one's lifestyle determines the destiny of one's spirit. If one goes to heaven, there is peace. However, unlike her, he does not believe that wicked spirits cuss, shoot, and fight each other in hell. Instead, they simply wander about without peace.

These testimonies conclude with a series of conjure and spirit stories by Mrs. Byrd's daughter, Ellen Lindsey:

I an't thought much 'bout conjure but I honesty believe I wuz hurt once myself. It wuz lak this. I use ter visit a friend 'oman in the rear of Third Street. One day when I wuz leavin her house, the 'oman that live next door ter her started in the door and we met. She grab both my hands and sed, "Come back into the house. I want to tell you something." So I followed her back in the room but she didn't tell me nothin instead she set there and stared at me lak she wuz crazy. Well I didn't think nothin' about it jest then. But later my hand, where she grabbed it, began ter swell up jest lak it would bust open. I went ter a doctor that wuz recommended by my employer, Mr. Boyston. This doctor gave me some liniment ter rub my hand with but it didn't get any better. Somebody told me about a old lady in Thomasville, that wuz called Ant Darkas, so I went ter see her. Ant Darkas looked at my hand then took it in hers. As she held my hand the swelling went from my hand in ter hers. I stayed out there three days and she would hold my hand 'til all the swelling left, then my hand busted and then it begin ter get alright. Later my employer told me this same 'oman came ter him and tried ter git my job, but they wouldn't have her. Now that's the trufe that 'oman did somethin ter my hand ter git my job.

During slavery time my mother went off ter a prayer meeting one night and left me ter care of the baby. After the baby went ter sleep I went next door till bed time. Well I sit there 'till I got sleepy and the 'oman come ter the door with me. I started across the yard and as I got ter the door

I heard something scratching all around the floor. I went on back, scared ter death, and got in the bed. Up in the loft I could hear those old hants saying, "cough, cough, cough," in a screechy voice and those in the room scratching all round the fireplace and going on jest lak a dog scratching. That house wuz in alarm that night some wuz a spittin and some wuz a coughing and some wuz a spittin. My pa had some whiskey there and I always believed they wuz looking fer that whiskey. They sed those old houses wuz built over the graves uv Indians. Many a night I have heard a chair in my room rocking. One night specially I heard that old rocking chair jest a rocking. I sed ter myself I go set up in bed and see what its go do, so I sets up and do you know that scoundrel stopped jest ez good 'till I layed down again. I jest wen't on ter sleep and let it rock all it wanted.

Then thar wuz the time old Mrs. Mims fell dead in the garden near our house. I sed, when I heard about it, "Well seems lak she coulda waited till she got in the house." After that if I would go out ter the wood pile at night something would always pull at my arm thinking I wuz going to run; but I nebber would run. Hants don't have no power so don't ebber run from 'em. I nebber will forgit anudder nite I had ter go down on the side by the hog pen and when I got gin the pen there wuz a knockin on the side that sounded lak a ax and when I looked I couldn't see a thing so thoughts come ter me that it wuz old lady Mim's spirit.[16]

Although Mrs. Byrd denies any real knowledge of conjure, her daughter, Ellen Lindsey, is an experienced believer. She is convinced that she herself was "hoodooed" through contagious magic and the "evil eye" by a woman who desired her job.[17] Traditional Western medicine was ineffective against this curse. So she turned to another female conjurer, Ant Darkas, who was able to cure her.[18]

Unlike Mr. Mobley, who doesn't believe in ghosts, Ellen does believe that while her mother was at a prayer meeting she received visitations from the "old hants" of dead Native Americans. In another account of an experience with a spirit, she expresses agitation over the fact that a neighbor, Mrs. Mims, did not die in her own home. Now, her spirit is wandering around theirs.

In these testimonies, the spectrum of beliefs ranges from denial to ambivalence to affirmation of the significance of spirits in the lives of slaves. Even in the story of Carrie Jones, a spiritual encounter provides the impetus for her conversion to Christianity. Like so many other conversion narratives, it is not simply through hearing a sermon that she comes to accept Christianity. Rather, it is the consequence of a direct experience with a spiritual presence in one form or another.[19] Even the apparition of Jesus on the wall is not too different from a typical hant experience. Phenomenologically, the two are very similar. This parallelism alone suggests a correlation in the slaves' mind between hants and the Spirit of Jesus. Later on, in the case of Mary Gladdy, we will see another example of this relationship between an experience with a ghost and a conversion to Christianity through the work of the Spirit.

The interweaving of non-Christian and Christian elements and the plurality of perspectives in these narratives are obvious. Like Ophelia, these narrators freely blend diverse beliefs into descriptions of their encounters with the spirits. For them, there is no single, unifying belief system. Within their stories one hears religious confessions that incorporate various traditions of African, European, and Native-American origin. What is more amazing though, is the absence of conflict among the witnesses. Although they may not agree, they are not concerned with invalidating each other's experiences or beliefs. Whether non-Christian or Christian, each perspective has its own validity within the African American experiences with the spirits and the Spirit.

However, there were other persons who did express conflicts between non-Christian beliefs and their Christian faith. Moreover, with respect to their Christian convictions, their testimonies reveal even deeper complications. Consider, for example, the case of Charlotte Sherold.

CHARLOTTE SHEROLD: SPIRITS, WHITE JESUS, BLACK DEVIL

Writer: "When is your church to have a revival, Charlotte?"

Charlotte: "We ain't goin' to have a revival 'til November, end of 'ear—look like the cullud people don't feel like prayin 'til the end of the 'ear. When you once get converted you just keep prayin'—and you get wisdom more and more—an it isn't anything hard."

Writer: "Do you believe in good and bad spirits?"

Charlotte: "That is, when you travelin'. When you first perverted (converted) you got to travel with good and bad spirits."

Writer: "Do you ever see spirits?"

Charlotte: "If you born with a caul, you see ghoses . . . sometimes your hair rises on your head."

Writer: "I wouldn't ask any good person if they believed in hags."

Charlotte: "But dat goin on right now; people say a hag ride me las' night."

Writer: "And what do you do for that?"

Charlotte: "Well ma'am, sprinkle roun' sulphur; we had a place like that and me husband burn sulphur, an we didn't have any more trouble. Good people don't have time for those things."

Writer: "Are you afraid to die?"

Charlotte: "No, ma'am, but I don't want to go before me time. My soul is nothin' but wind, and dat all we have. The frame is nothing."

The writer here told Charlotte about the "paly, green pastures," and asked her if she believed the Lord was a black man. She was both shocked and amused.

Charlotte: "How can we believe it; the Lord must be white, because I never saw any other kind of people rise and redeem!" Then Charlotte began to laugh: "If the Lord was a big black man, white people would sure haf to run from him—for I one would run from him." Charlotte continued, "God made two nations, the white and the black, and when we go to heaven we are all alike. These other nations are made by philosophers in other lands.

"We have a play in our church, 'Heaven Bound', and everybody dresses in white like angels—the devil is a black man dressed in red. I believe that if you go to the devil with badness, you get pitched over to the devil to stay."

Writer: "Does the devil make you work?"

Charlotte: "No, ma'am, you got to go in that fire and keep rolling over and over, burning."

Writer: "What do you think Heaven is like?"

Charlotte: "Heaven is everlasting rest."[20]

Charlotte Sherold, a former slave of Charleston, South Carolina, represents the deep tension some individuals experienced between non-Christian beliefs regarding the spirits and orthodox Christianity. Further, her testimony reveals an internalized hatred of her own ethnicity. In contrast to Phyllis (in the first narrative), she has no legend ("dem as could fly flew home") to recall as a challenge to her master's religion and culture. Instead, she believes that "Heaven is everlasting rest." At the same time, both Phyllis and Charlotte share a common vision of freedom from the cruelties of the present: one looks back toward a distant past, the other into a remote future. Thus, they both share the hope of freedom from present oppressions, far away from the toils of the plantation.

For Charlotte, the institutional church is where "cullud" people pray and have revival at the end of the year, that is, at the conclusion of the harvest season. Revival, Christian conversion, and prayer bring with them "wisdom more and more." Therefore, Christianity makes her life easier and eradicates the fear of death. At the same time, she does not want to die prematurely.

Like Amos, Ophelia, Mrs. Byrd, Mr. Mobley, and Ellen, Charlotte also acknowledges both the reality of spirits and the folklore surrounding them. She would agree that there are both good and bad spirits. She even offers a folk remedy for keeping the latter at abeyance. In the final analysis though, "good people don't have time for those things." In other words, they don't preoccupy themselves with such experiences.

However, at a deeper level, the most revealing dimension of Charlotte's belief system is her understanding of Jesus, heaven, hell, and the devil. The interviewer sets the context for this segment of the narrative by telling Charlotte about heaven ("the paly green pastures") and then proceeds to ask her if she believes the Lord is a black man. Charlotte is shocked, amused, and puzzled because white people are the only ones she has seen "rise and redeem"; they are the only ones who reap the benefits of Christianity. Therefore, Jesus also must be white. Otherwise, both white people and Charlotte herself would run away from him. However, the two nations "made" by God, that is, the white and the black, become one people in heaven. Somehow she believes that unity between the races, which cannot be achieved on this earth, is accomplished in heaven. As for other ethnic groups, they are left to their own philosophers; in other words, they have to discover their own path to salvation.

In Charlotte's church they have a play where everyone except the devil dresses in white "like angels." He poses as a black man in red. His sole purpose is to torment the wicked who burn in hell. Unlike Ophelia's vision of hell, this one does seem to be medieval: good and evil are separated by the stark hues of white and black. While Jesus cannot be black, the devil certainly is. With graphic images Charlotte is articulating a long-standing tradition of dualism within certain forms of Western mythological, philosophical, and theological thought.

Thus Charlotte's interpretation of the spiritual realm is more dualistic than syncretistic. She faces reality standing between toil and rest, good and bad spirits, good people and bad ones, a white nation and a black one, a white Jesus and a black devil, angels and a demon, and heaven and hell. It is difficult for her to hold these conflicting images together; they are polarized. If her testimony is the most Christian one examined so far, it is also one of the most dichotomous perceptions of reality. Consequently, her metaphors do not complement each other. Instead, they are held in an opposition that causes her to look forward to everlasting rest in heaven.

MARY GLADDY: SPIRIT-INSPIRED WRITING, SECRET MEETING

The next testimony comes from Muscogee County near Columbus, Georgia. It is the story of Mary Gladdy, who when asked how she had learned to write responds: "The Lord revealed it to me." It is the story of being "impelled" to do something forbidden by many masters during slavery. She received many visitations from the Spirit in the middle of the night and during these sessions, under the Spirit's inspiration, she wrote in ciphers. She is unable to translate some of these codes except through the same inspiration. More than forty years earlier Mary was converted to Christianity after a "hair-raising experience with a ghost." Like Carrie Jones in the story told by Henry Mobley, it was a spiritual encounter that caused this radical change.

Inteviewer: "When I asked her how she mastered this skill (that of writing), she replied: 'The Lord revealed it to me.' "

And indeed for more than thirty years the Lord has been revealing His Holy Word and many others to Mary Gladdy. For over twenty years she has been experiencing "visitations of the spirit." These do not occur with any degree of regularity, but they always come in "the dead hours of the night" after she has retired, and she is invariably impelled to rise and write in an unknown hand. Her strange writings now cover eight pages of letter paper and bear a marked resemblance to crude shorthand notes. Offhand she can "cipher" about half of these strange writings; the other half, however, she can make neither heads nor tails, except when the spirit is upon her. When the spirit eases off, she again becomes totally ignorant of the significance of the mysterious half of her spirit-directed writings. [21]

Her memories of religious worship during the Civil War are interesting and significant. In these difficult times, she says, it was customary among slaves to gather together secretly in their cabins two or three times each week and hold prayer and "experience" meetings. A large iron pot was always placed against the cabin door to keep the sound of their voices from escaping. Then slaves would sing, pray, and relate experience all night long. Their great soul-hungering desire was freedom. It was not that they loved the Yankees or hated their masters, she explained. They merely longed to be free and hated the institution of slavery.

Nearly always at these meetings every Negro attendant felt the spirit of the Lord "touch him just before day."[22]

Adjournment concluded with the following Old Slave canticle:

Jest befo' day, I feels 'im. Jest befo' day, I feels 'im.
My sister, I feels 'im. My sister, I feels 'im.
All night long I've been feelin' 'im.
Jest befo' day I feels 'im. Jest befo' day I feels 'im.
The sperit, I feels 'im. The sperit, I feels 'im.
(The second stanza substitutes the phrase, "my
    brother.")[23]

Mary's experience is reminiscent of the Jewish writers of the Hebrew Scriptures, who were inspired to record their experiences with their God. Like many of them, though for a different reason, she is driven to write much that she herself does not entirely understand. Whether or not her ciphers are intelligible is less important than the subversive activity she feels inspired to perform, that is, to write. This was prohibited by most slave masters with the threat of stern penalties. Nevertheless, it is precisely what she does under the compulsion of the Spirit. She chooses to exercise her freedom of self-determination in spite of what it might cost her. This is because she is willing to pay the "cost of discipleship."

It is significant to note that Mary is also a member of a community of faith. This, however, is not the formal church that some masters and slaves belonged to either together or separately. Also, it is not the year-end revival that Charlotte participated in. Rather, it is the secret meetings of the "Invisible Institution." These prayer and "experience" meetings, like Mary's compulsion to write, occur at night. In fact, they last all night long, under the guard of an iron pot, with singing, prayer, and testimony until "just before day," when Mary and others feel the Spirit. Their common objective is freedom. However, this is neither for the salvation of their souls, which they already have, nor for their rapture into heaven, which they anticipate, but for the deliverance of their bodies from physical oppression. Therefore, their experience of the Spirit is the impetus that inspires the desire for total liberation; it ignites the fires for freedom from slavery as a concrete objective to be achieved.

Evidently, for Mary and her community, their secret meetings provide them with the power of the Spirit through intercessory prayer which, in turn, enables them to overcome all forms of oppression. Since their prayer and "experience" meetings focus on freedom in this life, their Christian faith is not simply an escape from the harsh realities of their present condition. On the contrary, it inspires them to struggle against "the institution of slavery." By virtue of its secrecy, their meetings also are subversive forms of protest against the institutional churches mentioned above. These slaves are all "impelled" to find their own place where they can "sing, pray, and relate experiences all night long" until they feel the Spirit. Then they are inspired to struggle even more earnestly for their liberation.

RICHMOND ELLERBE: "STRUCK ME WIDE OPEN"

Many African American Christians not only felt the Spirit, but saw it, along with other visions, in ways that rival some of the best accounts of Western mystical experiences. Consider, for example, the testimony of "Doc" Richmond.

> Converted 73 years ago, Uncle Richmond or "Doc" was a preacher for 35 years.
> "When I was converted somthin' struck me wide open. I seed two men wid basin an' towel. Dey sey, 'You travlin' rite.' Dey hab a wide book, turn a leaf or two ober an' as dey 'gins to rite, I'se put back together an' am hole agin. Dey write my name in de book. Dey say, 'Go in peace an' sin no mo'. Yo' sins hab been forgiven.' I'se seen de Holy Spiret many times; I'se seen visions ob de green fiels ob edon, de people dere makin' happy move. An I'se seen the sinner, Hamp Pleasure, when he die. He say, 'Awe, Awe,' an' ring de roun's outer de chair fo he die."[24]

In the tradition of Johnson's *God Struck Me Dead*, "Doc" Richmond of Chesterfield, South Carolina, has a vision of himself being transformed from a sinner into a Christian. It is a typical African American conversion experience, an event accompanied by a radical encounter with spiritual beings. Although coming from a Christian, his testimony is not based totally upon assent to doctrinal accuracy. And yet, it contains many allusions to biblical symbolism.

This narrative blends both archetypal and biblical imagery into a coherent account of an African American conversion experience. On the one hand, Richmond utilizes archetypal metaphors that resonate with both Jungian analytical psychology and Eliadean phenomenology of religion: 1) the alchemical and/ or shamanistic process of disintegration and reintegration; 2) the presence of the two participant-witnesses; and 3) the symbolism of the basin, suggesting cleansing water. Likewise, both the book of life (and conversely of death) and the dual images of acceptance (Richmond, the Christian) and rejection (Hamp, the sinner) imply a symbiotic relationship between opposites, the *"mysterium conjunctionis."*[25] And further, this conversion process is even more significant when we consider that it initiates Richmond's call into the priesthood or ministry.[26] Overall, the form of this vision follows the classical pattern of a mystical-psychological experience of union with the divine.

On the other hand, the numinous quality of the vision itself contains several elements from biblical symbolism. First, there is the metaphor of traveling. As in the testimony of Charlotte Sherold, it refers to embarking upon a journey from a state of being a sinner to that of becoming a Christian; it is the exodus from the wilderness of sin to the New Jerusalem of salvation. Second, the basin and towel recall the Johannine account of Jesus washing his disciples' feet (Jn 13:5). Third, the men (or angels) examine the sinner and announce a declaration of pardon after recording his name in a book. Fourth, there is the book itself, an obvious reference to the "book of life" in Johannine apocalyptic literature (Rv 3:5; 13:8; 17:8; 20:12; 21:27). Fifth, the pronouncement, "Go in peace and sin no mo'. Yo' sin hab been forgiven," echoes Jesus' response to the woman caught in adultery (Jn 8:10, 11). And finally, the visions of the "Holy Spiret," "edon" (Eden), "de people dere makin' happy move" and the judgment of Hamp Pleasure constitute an interpretative synthesis drawn from various sources of the biblical narrative.

This utilization of biblical metaphors, and specifically apocalyptic ones, is dominant in many slave conversion experiences. It is peculiar given the fact that so many slaves were prohibited from reading the scriptures themselves. Often what they received were the highly selective catechisms from either their Euro-American masters and/or preachers to be obedient servants. When they were permitted to read the scriptures for themselves (or did so secretly), they gravitated toward those that called for a radical break from old patterns, both personal and social. Evidently the compelling power of the symbolism contained in such narratives spoke more readily to their existential situation as slaves, offering them hope for an uncompromising deliverance from sin and evil in all of their various forms.

It is also significant to note that "Doc" Richmond has "seen de Holy Spiret many times." This is not unlike the experience of other slaves' visions of the spirits. The spirits and the Spirit are experienced as they activate the senses of the recipient. Accordingly, they are not simply conceptualizations to be rationally understood. On the contrary, they are perceived and responded to as living phenomena. They are spoken of with symbols and metaphors intended to capture and convey as much of this experience as is linguistically possible.

BERLE AND MARIAH BARNES: "DE GRACE O' GOD"

Speaking of response, in the following testimony we encounter a profoundly unique one to the presence of the Spirit as a manifestation of "de grace o' God." It comes from Berle and Mariah Barnes, who live in the same region as Amos Long, that is, Seaboard, South Carolina. Mariah is the spokesperson in this narrative.

> I sets here 'mongst my rags and soot and gits so happy sometimes I jes 'bound to shout. I shouted de other night in bed. In de kitchen cookin' my little piece o' flour bread, in de gyarden workin' out my greens, in de bed—wherever de grace o' God swells up inside me I git so overjoyed I bound to praise my God. When was de las' time I shouted, old man?

> Well, Molly's gone now, but I's still here, and long as I feels de grace o' God in my heart I's goin' shout. De preacher is always glad to see me come to church.

"Grandma," he says to me, "we're gwine to have a good meetin' here to-day 'cause you come."

Now I and Berle is 83 apiece. I got high blood pressure. De doctor told me a summer ago not to shout no more, but when I feels de grace o' God steal over me I's gwine to praise my God, don't keer what de doctors say!

De slaves was all mighty proud to be free, mighty proud. Some of de marsters was good, and some was mean. Sometimes deye'd strip de slaves and whup deir backs till dey'd cut de blood out and den throw a bucket o' salt water over de raw backs. Dey made some of 'em plow all day and spin two ounces o' cotton at night. De slaves didn't git no flour bread, not even seconds; dey had to eat de grudgin's. And dey wa'n't 'lowed to meet to pray and shout neither; so dey'd have to slip off atter dark to one o' de houses and hold de prayer meetin's. Dey turned a big wash pot over close to de door, a little off'n de floor, so it'd ketch all de sound. Den de slaves'd shout and pray all dey pleased; every now and den one would slip out side to see if de pot was ketchin' all de sound. Sometimes when one would git so full o' the grace o' God and raise de shout too high, de other slaves'd throw him down on de bed and kiver up his head so he couldn't be hearn outside.

Me and de old man sets here and talks about de Bible and old times and what's gwine to 'come of us when de other one leaves here. Berle can read de Bible, but I wa'n't never learnt to read and write. Who was to blame for eatin' de apple dat time, old man? I forgits from one time to de next. How come Adam to blame? Cause de law was laid down to him, not to de woman; I 'members dat.

I been livin' close round Seaboa'd seventy year, but won't be many more days here for me. I's ready. I thinks about it most of de time now. Yes, mum, I studies more about gwine dan I does stayin.[27]

Although Mariah is sitting in the midst of "rags and soot," sometimes she gets so happy she cannot refrain from shouting. As represented by her testimony, this paradox of joy in the midst of sorrow suggests a theology of "de grace o' God." But since Mariah is illiterate, the grace of God and "shouting" have sustained her more on the basis of her direct experience of both God and human nature than on her indirect knowledge of either biblical or theological ideas.

Consequently, Mariah is an amazing example of the African American woman as a subversive religious leader in spite of traditional ecclesial restrictions against women preachers. Unlike "Doc" Richmond and her own pastor, there is no place in the church for her to assume leadership as a minister of the word. Nevertheless, since her presence in church ensures a "good meetin'," her leadership is somewhat acknowledged by her community of faith. At the same time, she realizes that it is Berle, the man, who can read the Bible and whose gender has determined the locus of sin to be in the woman. Applying her own "hermeneutics of suspicion," she raises the rhetorical question: "How come Adam to blame?" In response she replies, "Cause de law was laid down to him, not to de woman; I 'members dat." Thus, she offers an incisive critique of the traditional interpretation of the fall of humanity, which blames the woman. Furthermore, even though she cannot read the Bible, her description of slavery demonstrates that she has read the "text" of human nature very well.

In spite of her situation in the church, Mariah is a bearer of a tradition. She recounts both the sufferings (through punishments) and victories (through prayer and shouting), the perennial paradox of her people, in a style characteristic of women narrators. Consider, for example, her use of rhetoric to critique accepted authority combined with her sensitivity to the broader scope of humanity as viewed from the bottom up. Her "pulpit" is wherever she finds the opportunity to recall the struggles of her people under slavery.

According to Mariah's testimony, "Some of de masters was good, and some was mean." Sometimes slaves were stripped, beaten, tortured, overworked, and underfed. Moreover, they were not allowed to pray or shout. In other words, they were not allowed to commune with the Spirit for fear of what this might lead to, that is, the hunger and thirst for liberation. Like Mary Gladdy and her community, the community Mariah describes discovered the power of subversion. They mastered the techniques of secrecy in order to experience "de grace o' God," shout, and pray for freedom in their own space. On this latter point Mariah states unequivocally that: "De slaves was all mighty proud to be free, mighty proud."

In considering Mariah's testimony, it is also interesting to note that paradox is a prominent feature of many slave narratives. This sense of apparent contradiction and irrationality is pervasive. It raises some fundamental questions. For example, how could Mariah shout in the midst of rags and soot? And why would she intentionally ignore her doctor's warnings against shouting? Moreover, as she shares her testimony it is clear that the community she describes also lived in the midst of the sense of paradox. For instance, the whippings are held in tension with praying. Working all day is juxtaposed with slipping away at night to pray and shout in the presence of an iron pot that is supposed to muffle the ecstatic uproar generated by these secret meetings. In this sense we could say that the experience of paradox is the essence of "de grace o' God." Indeed, it is the *paradoxos*, a seemingly conflictual statement, that communicates what it means to rejoice – in spite of.

PHYLLIS GREEN: "RUSTYCATS," "WE CHURCH"

We will conclude the narration of these testimonies where it began, in Charleston, South Carolina, with Phyllis Green, a "low country Gullah negro."

Phyllis Green, a splendid type of the low country Gullah negro, described the services taking place in two churches that she passed on her way home as follows.

"You know when I come home an' pass dat church on de corner, I hear de poor choir dis strain so, an' aint a God's soul in dere to he'p em, an' when look an' saw 'nough of people to come out. I say, 'Do Jesus, is dat de best dey can do?' Dat church been full up wid rustycats [aristocrats]. Dem don't want to hear 'e boice [voice], but nebber mind when det [death] come den you hear dem sing. Dey dast not sing den. Den I gone on down de street an' pass an oder church. I could hear dat preacher mos' two blocks. I ain't mind hear em ef 'e stick to what 'e been wanna preach. 'E warn't any wishpering [whispering] preacher, an' dem does sing in dat church as sweet an' loud as any colored people.

"In we church we pray em for hear 'e boice. I aint mind ef 'e mash me foot, I can draw em enn (in) enty. I want en mash me foot ef I gib em 'casion."[28]

Phyllis recognizes three types of churches. First, there is the church of the "rustycats" (aristocrats), who are poor in the spirit. It is the one to which the wealthy and upper-middle-class Euro-American Christians belong, the Charleston elite. Only death causes them to sing loud and without restraint. Otherwise, in Phyllis's opinion, they strain to keep themselves under control. She wonders if Jesus or anyone else can help them out of their misery: "Do Jesus, is dat de best dey can do?" Second, there is the church of those people who sing just as "sweet an' loud as any colored people." In contrast to the "rustycats," the preacher in this church knows how to preach in a spirited manner. Furthermore, this choir is as good as her own. Unlike the first church, this one undoubtedly is composed of lower-class Euro-American Christians who are the offspring of the "Great Awakening" of Southern revivalism. And finally, there is "we church" for those African American slaves who could not fly back to Africa, but who could pray, sing, and shout as loud as they wanted to.

In Phyllis's church they pray in order to be heard both by God and their fellow worshipers. Moreover, if the Spirit moves someone in the congregation to "shout," it doesn't matter because Phyllis can always draw her feet in out of the way. Here there is no need to be concerned with dignity and restraint because the Spirit has full control within this context of prayer and worship. On the one hand, they experience the freedom of total self-expression. On the other hand, there is full communal participation. Unlike the "rustycats," singing is not limited to the choir. But also unlike the other church down the street, the preacher and choir are not the only ones who may raise their voices in worship. Here, they can all shout as loud as the Spirit inspires them.

In the legend of Solomon Legare Island, would-be African American slaves flew back directly to Africa because they refused to accommodate themselves to their new environment. Phyllis remembers this story as an example of resistance to the religion and lifestyle of her mistress. Apparently her own situation dictated a different response; she became a Christian. Nevertheless, her experience of the Christian faith, as reported in this testimony, is very different from her Euro-American counterparts. For her, the phenomenon of African American spirituality transforms a Eurocentric Christianity into a religion that is unique to her own community of faith. Thus, under the constraints of personal, social, and economic oppression, it continually gives her something to shout about.

SUMMARY

In these narratives African American slaves encounter the spirits and the Spirit through dreams, visions, and other phenomena. Often these experiences are reinforced through their folklore. Some of these beliefs are similar to traditional African religions. Others represent a syncretism of African, European, and Native American beliefs. For many African American slaves who consider themselves to be Christian, there is no sense of contradiction or dualism between their experiences of the spirits and the Spirit.

Some of the beliefs of traditional African religions are transformed through the influence of Christianity, especially Protestantism.[29] Nevertheless, the spirits remain close in the imagination of Southern slaves through folklore and experiences of ghosts, witches, talking animals, and other supernatural phenomena.[30] The imagination of the slaves is filled with images of the supernatural, both non-Christian and Christian. They are moved and animated by these numinous encounters that affect them physically as well as emotionally and psychologically. Accordingly, they recount these experiences through symbols and metaphors that re-create their encounters.

Within the context of communal worship, slaves are free to

express themselves without inhibitions. Since they are away from the suspicious gaze of their masters, this worship experience is often accompanied with hand-clapping, foot-tapping, and, when possible, the beating of drums or the sounds of other musical instruments.[31] Once they feel the Spirit, they enter another dimension.

So, many slaves adopted the outward appearance of Christian conversion while they interpreted this religion very differently from their masters, and thus were inspired to rebellion. Others used this new religion to adjust themselves better to their condition of servitude. However, they all discovered ways of describing religious experiences that were liberating within the conditions they lived under. I maintain that much of this occurred through their masterful use of metaphors. Now let us turn to consider some hermeneutical implications of African American slave narratives, both non-Christian and Christian, for a contemporary black theology of liberation.

SOME HERMENEUTICAL IMPLICATIONS

These testimonies from slave experiences of non-Christian and Christian experiences of the spirits and the Spirit are intended to illustrate a significant contribution to a contemporary black theology of liberation: the incorporation of the diversity and totality of the religious experiences of African American slaves into a theology based on their testimonies. Moreover, its theological constructions should be influenced by new insights gained from the symbols and metaphors used by slaves themselves in describing their religious experiences.

At the outset of this chapter, I stated that I would utilize insights from the writings of Paul Ricoeur with respect to: 1) the task of hermeneutics; 2) the importance of symbolic and metaphorical language; 3) the function of the narrative genre; and 4) the appropriation of what the text presents. In the preceding section, I attempted to place the texts in front of the reader and allow them to guide my interpretations. Certainly, the ones I have offered are not the only possibilities. As I see it, these narratives or testimonies are extended metaphors that avail themselves to multiple interpretations.[32] Nevertheless, the major point I have sought to underscore is that African American slave narratives, both non-Christian and Christian, should evoke theological insights from their own language. Their very nature, which is metaphorical, gives us rich material to interpret. Once we understand the slaves' uses of language we may proceed to engage in a constructive theological reflection on their significance from our own perspective. At this juncture let me briefly outline my own hermeneutical proposal in relation to African American slave narratives and a contemporary black theology of liberation. As I mentioned before, since this essay is primarily concerned with hermeneutical implications, a fuller treatment of specific theological themes will be the task of a future project.

THE PRIMARY TASK OF HERMENEUTICS

We encounter the reality of the slaves through the texts of their narratives. This presents us with the primary task of hermeneutics, that is, the engagement in the operations of the interpretation of texts.[33] It is the process of coming to understand the reality of slaves through their testimonies as mediated through their stories and of being affected by their transformative power. Hermeneutics seeks to draw our attention to the "world of the text" — a description of the slaves' experiences — and enables us to participate in that world through our imagination and become reoriented in our own present situation. Through symbol, metaphor, and narrative, the text invites us to come to understand the reality of African American slaves and discover new meaning from it for our own circumstances. Thus, a hermeneutics of slave narratives should bring us to a place where our world (existential situation, preunderstanding, volitional faculties) is opened up to the new possibilities presented by the world of the text which, in turn, we appropriate as our own. Therefore, in order to fully appreciate Amos Long's belief in Mis' Marthy's return from the dead and its moral consequences, we have to enter into the world his story presents. Then we can appropriate the warning to remember one's heritage. The same is true for comprehending the impact of Ophelia Jemison's subtle critique of her interviewer's inquiry regarding "bad sperrits." Her response presupposes familiarity with an Afrocentric understanding of the roles of different kinds of spirits, even within a Christian interpretation of reality.

When considering texts from a different historical period than our own, a further challenge for hermeneutics or interpretation is to overcome the distance in time and culture.[34] Consequently, when interpreting African American slave narratives we are compelled to translate the language arising from their historical, cultural, social, economic, and religious setting into one that speaks to us now. In other words, hermeneutics should enable us to hear the contemporary message of liberation coming from the texts of a different place and time. Slave narratives are made contemporaneous once they are understood as presented in the text and then translated into modern speech. Our task is that of coming to understand how slaves both understood and communicated their experiences and struggles through their use of language; that is, the symbolic and metaphorical language of African American slaves becomes clear to us through our repeated exposure to the way they transform their experiences into images that tell their stories of both oppression and liberation. In the final analysis, hermeneutics involves the utilization of a creative imagination that culminates in our appropriation of a world projected through the text. This is the end result of an interpretative process. Through a cycle of orientation (reading the text), disorientation (becoming disturbed by what we read), and reorientation (making a decision to act on the basis of what we have read), we come to realize a fuller self as a new world of possibilities is appropriated.[35] Consequently, the world of the slave is translated into language that is meaningful for our contemporary experiences and struggles in the process of achieving liberation from all contemporary forms of individual and social oppression.

THE IMPORTANCE OF SYMBOLIC AND METAPHORICAL LANGUAGE

Slave narratives speak to us through symbols and metaphors that redescribe the experiences of African American people under slavery. This calls our attention to the importance of symbolic and metaphorical language. Language is not a world, but since we are in the world and have something to communicate to others, we express ourselves through language.[36] Moreover, it empowers us to create metaphors for describing our experiences. Historically, the oral tradition of African American slaves placed a high value upon the power of speech. It was evocative, driving internal mental, emotional, and spiritual experiences into the exterior reality of the African American slave. Transformation (for example, through either a non-Christian religious experience of possession or an Afrocentric Christian conversion) of the individual was often accomplished through the spoken word (either non-Christian exhortation or Christian preaching), along with music, dancing, shouting, and so on. Moreover, all of this was usually related to an encounter with either spirits or God, Jesus, and the Spirit. Therefore, language as oral discourse was the primary mode of expression for communicating internal experiences.[37] For African American slaves, the oral tradition was also the primary medium for creating their own reality. This new reality was separate from that of their masters (as professed Christians) and the one that had been assigned to them by their masters (as persons who had been converted to Christianity). In sum, symbolic language empowered African American slaves to define their own relationships with the spirits, God, and other human beings.

With respect to African American slave narratives, symbolic language is significant because it speaks a creative word to the "mythicopoetic" center of our imagination.[38] In other words, symbolic language is rooted in the core of how we understand ourselves and the world around us. And further, it engages our imagination and reveals human possibilities beyond present realities.[39] There are at least three implications from this concept that are noteworthy for a hermeneutics of slave narratives.

First, symbolic language should be studied in terms of its structure, its functioning. Unlike logical, rational, univocal language (for example, that of science), it has the power to awaken the imagination and renew myths.[40] That is, it lends itself to creative, poetic communication between persons. In the case of African American slave narratives, this can function not only in terms of "wishful thinking," but also as willful visioning. Consider, for example, the diverse functions of symbolic language in the testimonies of Phyllis Green, Charlotte Sherold, Mary

Gladdy, and Richmond Ellerbe. Phyllis recounts a legend of returning to Africa. Charlotte sees heaven as a place of rest. Mary has the gift of writing "revealed" to her. And Richmond has a vision of personal transformation. In each case the metaphors they use express not only wishful thinking, but also a determination to dream of and hope for a better life, both literally and symbolically, beyond their present situation under slavery.

Second, the symbolic activities of thinking and of speaking prolong the power to dream. Since symbols are bound to language, they enable us to speak poetically about our experiences through concrete ("opaque") images in lieu of rational conceptualizations. Thus the symbols and metaphors of slaves "make sense" when read symbolically (but with reference to concrete experiences). Such is the vision of Richmond Ellerbe's conversion; the images are as concrete and vivid as the experience was for him. It should be added that all symbolic language says something other than what it seems to. The direct meaning conceals an indirect one; what is implied may be more important than what is expressed verbally. Symbols have multiple layers of meaning. Likewise, symbolic language is inexhaustible; it too has an excess or "surplus of meaning."[41] One commonplace example of this in slave narratives is the development of "gospel spirituals," which also were sung as codes for plans of escape from the plantation (for example, songs like "Steal Away to Jesus"). In a similar vein the Old Slave Canticle recorded in Mary Gladdy's testimony is a witness to the social and political liberating power of the Spirit; it is much more than a mere personal and pietistic affirmation of faith.

And finally, symbolic language, being deeply rooted within the psyche, is immediately recognizable, even though it still has to be interpreted. It strikes an intuitive precognition which, in turn, should be deciphered and understood. In other words, like the symbol it also evokes interpretation.[42] Thus, when we approach slave narratives we are sensitive to the fact that their messages both reveal and conceal protests against slavery. This is why Mariah Barnes can reassure us that despite all appearances of contentment, the slaves were "mighty proud to be free."

THE FUNCTION OF THE NARRATIVE GENRE

The third major insight to be gained from a hermeneutics of African American slave narratives is the perception that the narratives tell their stories. To put it differently, slave narratives communicate by developing a plot. This underscores their function as a narrative genre. As a medium for storytelling, the poetic function of language re-creates and redescribes reality. In the case of the slave narratives we are considering, something is being said about the slaves' experiences with spirits and the Spirit. Furthermore, they are sharing their experiences under slavery with us. One of our tasks is to discover that reality as presented in the text by paying close attention to how distinct symbols and symbolic language are transformed into a coherent system. This happens through emplotment and narrativity.

Emplotment is the arrangement of different factors (events, circumstances, characters, and so forth) into a meaningful synthesis in order to relate a story, and in order that the text might be considered as a whole.[43] Hence, the story conveyed is a human product that helps us understand someone else's experience. The slaves' experience of slavery and of religious encounters are shaped into a story intended to communicate their desire for a better life both here on earth and beyond death. Moreover, all of their stories of encounters with spirits and the Spirit are related because they create powerful images and impressions that reach beyond their own physical, social, political, and economic limitations as slaves. Most often the plot or story line draws together both non-Christian and Christian themes around a common motif. A case in point is the testimonies of Mrs. Byrd, Henry Mobley, and Ellen Lindsey. Their stories combine beliefs in root medicine, conjure, and spirits with Christianity. But more than that, these witnesses create a common plot or theme around their various beliefs regarding spirits. This becomes their shared narrative and gives us, the readers, a fuller picture of their world-view.

Narrativity relates to the overall effect of a text as a literary genre or type of literature, for example, as either a historical or poetic document.[44] It includes the entire range of semantic codes incorporated into the development of the story. In brief, it controls the organization of events (related and/or not) into a meaningful whole; the beginning and ending of these events; and the representation of time as moving from a past or present into a future. Moreover, it combines chronological and episodic events into a story or narrative.[45] Phyllis Green's account of the Africans who could fly home is an example of the most pervasive African American story that blends the elements mentioned above into an impressive, coherent narrative. It should be noted that many people throughout the Carolinas and Georgia believed this phenomenon as an oft-repeated historical event, not merely as a myth. By reading a text, a narrative engages our imagination as we seek to live in a world initially foreign to us. As we read the narratives of African American slaves, a world unfolds before us. It is one that gives us a window for viewing both the oppression of slavery and the struggle for liberation. As historical and poetic documents these stories generate plots (emplotment) and develop narratives (narrativity) for creatively communicating facts about the joys and sorrows of slaves. Consequently, along with slave folklore, spirituals, and so on, slave narratives reveal both the world they lived in as well as the one they hoped for. Moreover, they present us with the same alternative of living in the present while striving for a better future. In the final analysis we must choose which proposal to appropriate and act upon; we must decide how to translate their message into thoughts and actions that are relevant for our own situation. We must ask ourselves how the symbolic and metaphorical language of these narratives inspires and guides our own struggle for a richer, fuller, more liberated life. Ultimately we have to ask ourselves how their testimonies will inspire us to seek liberation from various forms of oppression.

APPROPRIATION OF THE WORLD OF THE TEXTS

Slave narratives present a world we may either appropriate or reject. Herein lies their transformative power for our own situation. Interpreting a text should result in self-interpretation, a better self-understanding, and indeed, a fuller, richer self through the appropriation of its proposed world.[46] When we make ourselves available to the proposed world of African American slave narratives, we assume the risk of being transformed through their messages. But how can the symbolic language, emplotment, and narrativity of these stories empower us in this process? I offer three suggestions.

First, their symbolic language speaks to our mythicopoetic core, thus engaging our imagination in a creative conversation with the signs and codes of their texts. Second, we are compelled first to "explain" (by becoming familiar with the slaves' use of language) and then "understand" (by translating their language into our own) the narratives through their story.[47] The slaves' stories are the organization of distinct symbols into symbolic systems that express both their resistance to bondage and desire for freedom. And finally, their narratives tell a story that presents a world we may choose to enter into and, ultimately, appropriate.

But it is also a world we may choose to reject. Our appropriation of the testimonies of African American slaves does not allow us to remain neutral or objective. We soon discover that their language redescribes their reality at many levels. African American slaves used symbols and metaphors to define their own reality as distinct from the one that had been imposed upon them by their masters. While striving for social and political freedom, they also fought for linguistic liberation, that is, for self-expression. This is the leitmotif in all of the testimonies from Phyllis Green to Mary Gladdy to Mariah Barnes. Through narratives, folklore, spirituals, and so forth, African American slaves liberated themselves from having their voices silenced by illiteracy. In spite of this limitation in a society that glorified literacy, they created through their own metaphorical language limitless "worlds" we may appropriate into a contemporary black theology of liberation.

In sum, to place ourselves in front of the text of African American slave narratives is to expose ourselves to their symbolic-poetic world. To appropriate this reality is to engage our imagination in the revelation of a possible world and the advancement toward a new way of existing in this world. By stepping toward the so-called primitive, primordial, and archetypal world of the African American slave, we might be able to hear a renewed word on how to find meaning in apparently meaningless situations as we come to realize our larger selves through the symbols, metaphors, parables and poetry of their testimonies.

Summary

I would suggest that a major focus of a contemporary black theology of liberation should be on how the symbols and metaphors used by slaves can enhance the praxis of liberation on the hermeneutical, linguistic-poetic front as well as in the political, social, and economic struggle for full humanity. In other words, the symbols and metaphors used by African American slaves to describe their reality should further inspire us to borrow more from them in constructing a contemporary black theology of liberation. In this regard the expression, "coming through 'ligion," may be thought of as a heuristic metaphor that implies an engaging process for black theologians in developing a constructive theology from the testimonies of African American slaves. We also should ask ourselves if we are willing to assume the risk of being surprised by what we have yet to discover as we continue to "come through" their testimonies.

In order to speak of a contemporary black theology that is in conversation with the narratives of African American slaves, we should first learn the language of those narratives. Then we can interpret them and translate their meaning into one of our own. I am convinced by this preliminary hermeneutical undertaking that there is much to be gleaned from a more rigorous study of these narratives. In contrast to a condescending evaluation that would consider African American slave testimonies as expressions, to use a biblical analogy, "of ignorant and unlearned [people]" (Acts 4:13), this assessment suggests that African American slaves utilized the linguistic resources made available to them as masters and mistresses of symbols and metaphors. If we are willing to hear their voices, some of our contemporary paradigms for doing theology, like the image of "Doc" Richmond undergoing a transformation, may be "struck wide open."

4

LIBERATION ETHICS
IN THE EX-SLAVE INTERVIEWS

CHERYL J. SANDERS

The ex-slave interviews provide day-to-day moral data that can be used to analyze the ethical perspectives of the ex-slaves. Many of them testified of the experience of conversion, understood here as a conscious moral change from wrong to right, involving reorientation of the self from complacency or error to a state of right religious knowledge and action. Ethics evaluates human actions, character, and institutions in terms of good and evil, right and wrong. The experience of conversion can influence an individual's social ethical perspectives in concert with the changes in personal morality. The conversion experience did not alter a slave's status legally or otherwise. Like all slaves, those who converted to Christianity were subjected to a broad range of life experiences in slavery.

If conversion caused a significant reorientation of the self in moral terms, what, if any, ethical realignments did conversion produce in the converts' attitudes toward slavery? How were the social and religious ethics of the converted slaves related with reference to the problem of slavery? Did the experience of conversion generate a liberation ethic among the slaves? These questions will guide the explorations and investigations of this chapter; the goal is to produce a critical analysis of the moral reflections and ethical styles of a select group of ex-slaves who had been converted while in slavery. A paradigm developed by ethicist Ralph Potter will be used as an interpretive tool applied to ethical statements made by ex-slaves. Potter's paradigm searches out four essential elements in an ethical statement: 1) empirical definition of the situation; 2) affirmation of loyalty; 3) mode of ethical reasoning; and 4) quasi-theological beliefs concerning God, humankind, and human destiny.[1] The power of this interpretive tool rests in its usefulness in clarifying the disagreements that arise among various parties in relation to a particular ethical issue by discerning the various patterns of moral discourse they pursue in light of their empirical definitions, affirmations, and beliefs.

Four ex-slave interviews have been selected for special analysis from the thousands of oral histories collected during the 1920s and 1930s and subsequently edited and published during the 1970s by George P. Rawick under the title *The American Slave: A Composite Autobiography*.[2] They were chosen on the basis of three criteria: 1) an explicit testimony of conversion to Christianity; 2) extensive ethical reflection upon the problem of slavery; and 3) diversity of experience of and attitudes toward slavery. There are two men and two women: Pet Franks, age 92, of Monroe County, Mississippi; Sister Kelly, age unknown, of Nashville, Tennessee; Wesley Little, age 85, of Smith County, Mississippi; and Laura Redmoun, age 82, of Dallas, Texas. At the time of the interview, Franks was employed as a cook at a local fishing lodge. Kelly was disabled, but offered no indication of her current source of support. Little, retired from farming and preaching, lived on a government pension. Redmoun also received a government pension and supplemented her income by doing laundry for a white family.

Pet Franks was born in Mississippi to Martha and Martin Franks, slaves who had been brought there from Virginia. Franks grew up and worked on a large plantation, both in the fields and around the house. Religious meetings were held on the plantation for the slaves. Franks's own conversion experience occurred as he was being baptized in the Mississippi River. Franks worked as a waiter and nurse in a Confederate Army camp during the Civil War, but returned to the plantation prior to the end of the war to look after his master's wife and children. He stayed with his former owners-employers after freedom. Franks married Dora Franks (who also was interviewed), another former slave, shortly after freedom, and the two of them had eight children, three of whom were living at the time of the interview. He and Dora had been separated for twenty-three years at the time of the interview, because they could not get along with each other, and because he wanted to move away from the town of Aberdeen (where they had lived together) to the country in order to work in the fishing lodge.

Sister Kelly makes no mention of her parents or of the circumstances of her birth. She does recall that her master was dead by the time she was old enough to know things, and that her mistress, Mary Brook, hired an overseer and guardians to manage the slaves. She worked as a field hand on her mistress's plantation. However, she was hired out as a house servant after her mistress's death. Sister Kelly had a dramatic conversion experience at the age of 12. It began on a Sunday morning with the onset of uncontrollable crying. She asked her employer to let her go home to the Brook plantation. Upon returning home, and as she continued to cry, her mistress asked what was the matter with her, and she said she didn't know. She went from there to a flat place near a pond, where she began to hear voices. She shouted and prayed and cried, and fasted for three days and three nights. An older slave, Aunt July, counseled her to pray. The voice, which she identified as coming from the Lord, kept speaking to her and exhorting her to believe as she overcame her initial ignorance of what was happening and how to pray. Eventually she found the grace she had been seeking and a feeling of being made brand new. By the time of the Civil War, Sister Kelly was married to Jim Kelly and had three children. She claims to have witnessed the last battle that took place in Nashville. She does not discuss the end of the war or her emancipation from slavery, but she says that she returned to the plantation after her husband died. No explanation is offered of how or why she came to Nashville, where she lived at the time of the interview, nor of her past or present sources of support.

Wesley (or Westly) Little lived for all his life within two and one-half miles of his birthplace. He makes no mention of his mother, but recalls that his father was also born in Mississippi and belonged to a German who failed in his attempts at farming. The German sold all his slaves to a small farmer by the name of Little. Little's father escaped in the midst of the sales transaction and later joined the Union Army. Little recalls that he received some early religious and secular education from his mistress. As a child he was converted by a sermon preached in a white church, but failed to go forward when the minister issued the invitation to join the church to the slaves seated at the rear. However, he confided in his mistress concerning his desire to join, and she encouraged him to take steps to do so the next time. When he got older, he worked as a field hand. After the Civil War, he and his family left his former owners and settled on a small farm. He married twice (his first wife died) and raised two sets of children. He received a call to preach and responded by attending school with his children. After acquiring this educational instruction, Little served as an itinerant preacher for twenty years. During the Depression he became disabled and lost his home but was able to apply for a government pension with the help of a local white man.

Laura Redmoun was enslaved as an urban house servant in Memphis, Tennessee. She was born a twin on a plantation in nearby Jonestown. Her only knowledge of her parents was gained after freedom, when her mother came to live with her in response to an advertisement Redmoun placed in the newspapers. Redmoun does not indicate that she ever knew what happened to her twin brother. At the age of 6 months she was given as a wedding present to the daughter of her original owners. Redmoun was taken to Memphis when her mistress moved there with her husband. There was only one other slave in the household, who worked as a cook. As a child, Redmoun went with her mistress to church and usually slept at her feet. When she was 8, she began to listen to preaching and soon had an ecstatic conversion experience. She ran away for three days and was found by a group of men on horseback, who returned her to her mistress. Redmoun's mistress did not allow her to be whipped for running away. Instead, she counseled Redmoun to "calm down" so that she could be in a "fit condition" to join the church. She had the cook take Redmoun to a Baptist church and allowed her to join at the age of 9. Redmoun was baptized in the Mississippi River at about the same time federal troops entered Memphis, and Redmoun helped her mistress hide her jewelry and silverware. Redmoun claims that emancipation meant nothing to her, because she never knew that she was a slave. She stayed with her former mistress after freedom. When Redmoun was 17, her former mistress died. She wanted Redmoun to be married before she died, so the wedding ceremony was performed at the mistress's deathbed. Redmoun continued to work for whites as she and her husband farmed. All six of their children died in infancy. Eventually they moved to Texas, where she lived as a widow at the time of the interview.

EMPIRICAL DEFINITION OF THE SITUATION

Given that these four ex-slaves had vastly different life experiences as slaves, it would be reasonable to expect their empirical definitions of the problem of slavery in ethical terms to reflect a similar degree of diversity. For each of them, the principal sources of empirical information are personal experiences and firsthand knowledge of the experiences of other slaves.

Pet Franks claims to be quite knowledgeable about slavery, and his empirical assessments of the institution are positive:

> I knows all about slavery and de war. I was right dere on the spot when it all happened. I wish to goodness we was back dere now, not in de war but in de slavery times. Niggers where I lived didn't have nothin' to worry bout in them days.[3]

In his view, slavery provided a carefree existence for the slaves. The generosity of his former owners apparently created pleasant living conditions for the slaves, who were also allowed to reap the benefits of their own industriousness and initiative:

> All de niggers on de Tatum place had dey own patches where dey could plant what ever dey wanted to and dey could work dey patch on Satdays. When dey could sell anything from dey patch de mistress would let dem keep

de money dey got for it and when de boats went down to Mobile we could send down for anything we wanted to buy. One time I had $10.00 saved up and I bought lots of pretties with it. We allus had plenty to eat too. All de greens, de eggs, wheat, corn and meat dat you could want. And when hog-killin' time would come we'd allus have some meat left over from de year befo' and we'd take dat and make soap out of it.[4]

Franks's only negative statements concerning slavery are offered with reference to slaves from other places. He says that he heard of slaves on other plantations being whipped. He witnessed firsthand the case of a slave who died of exposure in the winter, and also that of a slave who was brutally tortured by his master for expressing a desire for the Yankees to win the war so that he could be free. His assessments of the institution of slavery seem to focus on the moral differences between whites. He describes his owners as good white folks and even extends this same evaluation to the overseer:

We had a good overseer, his name was Marse Frank Beeks and he was as fine a white man as ever lived. I doan never 'member him whippin' one of his niggers, leastways not real whippin's.[5]

Thus Franks's empirical definition of the problem of slavery rests upon the idea that slavery was a good thing when administered by good whites. He saw morally conscientious whites as being in a position to use the law to check the abuses of immoral whites. Throughout his narrative Franks is careful to identify himself with whites. It is evident that both in slavery and in freedom he has been dependent upon benevolent whites for his livelihood.

Sister Kelly formulates a radically different empirical definition of the problem of slavery. She regards herself as particularly knowledgeable about the hardships of slavery:

If you wants me to tell you what a hard time the po' ole slave had working and gitting whupped, and sech like that,

I knows about that, yessir, and I ain't forgot neither. I
never will forget none of that this side of the grave. I have
plowed many a field, honey. Sometime, we was in the field
time it was daylight, and sometime even before day broke;
we would work there all day, then we had to shell corn at
night when it was too dark to bend yo' back any longer in
the field.[6]

In Kelly's view, the institution of slavery was built on an
immoral foundation of hatred, deprivation, theft, and economic
gain. She describes her former mistress as good, but applies the
term *good* to whites with a high degree of skepticism:

Well, she was good as most any old white woman. She was
the best white woman that ever broke bread, but you know,
honey, that wasn't much, 'cause they all hated the po' nigger. When she died she said the only reason she hated to
die was on account of her children; didn't say a word 'bout
her po' slaves what had done wuked theyselves to death
for her.[7]

Thus, the goodness of whites, even the best of them, is
negated by their hatred of blacks. Notwithstanding the injustice
of having been forcibly overworked, Kelly resents her mistress's
total lack of gratitude and appreciation for the labors of her
slaves. The slaves suffered deprivations that were attributable
to the sheer meanness of whites:

You know when I come along we didn't know our ages nor
nothing. They stole just like they stealed now, times ain't
changed much, and people ain't changed none. ... The
white folks throwed the book what had our ages in it in
the fire to keep us from having it, and none of us never
knowed just how old we was.[8]

Kelly condemns the economic motive that undergirded slavery based on her own experience of having been hired out: "I
was hired out: I was 'bout 13 years old then. Yes, you know
white folks is always after the money."[9] The system of hiring out

provided for the owner of a slave to gain income by "renting" the slave to another employer in an arrangement where the wages would be paid to the owner instead of to the slave. Because wages were withheld from the slaves who worked to earn them, the hiring-out system is regarded by Kelly as a form of theft. Kelly remembers Christmas holidays as "fine times" for the whites, but "awful" for the blacks being hired out:

> When Christmas come, we would come home; all the white folks would come from New York and places, and ther was sho' nuf fine times, I tell you. Them ole red headed yaps would bid us off to the highest bidder and we couldn't do nothin' but pray. Yes, fine times for them, but awful for us po' niggers. Yes'm, they would cry you off to the highest bidder for the next year. One by one, we had to get up on that block, and he bid us off.[10]

Kelly does not identify at all with whites; in her opinion the lines remained clearly drawn between whites and blacks in the slave system. Her empirical definition of the problem of slavery holds that it was an evil system that fostered the economic interests of the white slave holders at the expense of blacks and sanctioned racial hatred. For blacks, slavery was an experience of poverty, deprivation, and economic injustice. The slaves' only hope rested in their prayers to God for deliverance.

Wesley Little was a slave from birth to the age of 19. He never ventured more than a "stone's throw" from the places where he lived and worked as a slave. Not sharing his father's desire to escape from slavery to fight with the Union Army, Little remembers slavery times as "de good ole days."[11] His endorsement of slavery is based on the perception that the slaves were well-treated, properly disciplined, and enjoyed their labors. The care of the slaves was directly supervised by a "good" master:

> Dis may not sound lak slaves days but I had a good master what sho' 'nuf looked after us in de right way. I wuz fed jes' lak marse wuz, de same kind o' food dat him an' his folks et, an' we wuz sat down to a table o' plenty. Our

cabins wuz small but big 'nuf fer us 'cause all our cookin' an' eatin' went on at Marse's. Us had big fire places wid plenty o' fat pine an' logs to burn, an' when hit wuz even a bit chilly us had a roarin' fire. Us had good beds to sleep on an' plenty o' kiver. Marse worked us reasonably too, an' since he didn't hab slaves 'nuf to keep a over seer an' done de over seein' his self deir wuz very little whippin' gwine on.[12]

Little's master took steps to provide for the religious, moral and educational development of his slaves, although it was his mistress who gave him guidance in his own conversion experience. Little is particularly grateful for the two whippings he received as a boy from his master for stealing and for carelessness, because he learned honesty and integrity as a result of the whippings and the talks that came with them. With reference to slave labor, Little claims that the slaves enjoyed picking cotton:

I plowed wid de slaves, hoed, an picked cotton. We laked cotton pickin' times. A bunch ob us in a big white fiel' ob cotton whar we could pick an' sing an' joke one another. We knowed plenty to eat wuz waitin' fer us an' a good nights sleep. Give a darkie dat an' he can be happy as a coon.[13]

Little recalls having identified very closely with whites, especially during childhood:

I played wid Marse chillun lak I did my own brothers an' sisters. A heap o' nights after we had played hard all day an' until late I has crawled in de bed wid Marse's boys an' slept all night.[14]

Ironically, he identifies positively with the success of the native-born Southern planters, who made their fortunes using slave labor (in contrast to the "strangers" who came to the South and failed as farmers, like the German who owned his father): "It takes us ole southerns to know how to make dis good lan' yield."[15]

In Little's opinion, freedom was more of a problem in the South than slavery. He shows some regret that the freed slaves were never given the land and provisions promised them so that they could make a living for themselves, but at the same time he justifies the Ku Klux Klan's use of terrorist tactics to subjugate blacks:

> When de war come on we wuz tole lan' an' stuff would be give us. We didn't know much what to believe. Hard an' turrible times followed. Food an' clo'es got mighty scarse. . . . When de war did end de slaves wuz turnt loose wid no way to take care o' dem selves. An' to cap hit all de Ku Klux sprung up a whippin' an' a meddlin' up wid everything. But you couldn't blame de white folks from clannin' up cause de freed niggers got might smart an' hard headed. Dey thought dey owned everything jes' 'cause dey wuz free.[16]

When taken at face value, Little's statements lead to the conclusion that he experienced and evaluated slavery in empirical terms as a "good" institution under the administration of "good" whites. Moreover, he holds that honesty, integrity, racial harmony, and other moral virtues that were preserved under the slavery system were overturned in freedom.

Laura Redmoun's narrative opens with a proud declaration of the maternal bond that existed between her mistress and her during slavery:

> The funny thing 'bout me is, I was a present to the white folks right off. They was looking for my little old mammy to have a baby a bless God I was born twins. They was two of me, a boy and a girl. Then when I was six months old Miss Gusta, my old mistress' daughter (Old Mis' Roberston) married Mr. Scruggs and then old Mis' gave me to Miss Gusta for a weddin' present.
>
> Miss Gusta was proud of me like I had been her own little baby. I slep' right on the feet of her bed.[17]

Redmoun does not mention doing any work as a slave, implying that she was actually kept as a pet. In fact, she denies ever knowing that she was a slave: "Then Miss Gusta tol' me I wan't no slave no more but shux that don't mean nothin' to me. 'Cause I ain't never knowed I was one."[18] Although she claims to have had no concept of herself as a slave, she mentions that slavery was a cruel experience for her mother. After freedom Redmoun sought and found her mother in a "pitiful condition."

> I advertised roun' in the papers and found my mammy and she came and lived with me. She was in a pitiful condition. Before the ceasin' of the war her master sold her and the man what bought her wan't so light on his niggers. She said they made her wear britches and tote big heavy logs and plow with oxes. Once they went to whup her and she fit them back and it took two men to hold her. She scratched and bit. One of the mens knocked her on the back of the head with a club and from that day she always shook her head from side to side all the time like she couldn't get her mind straight.
>
> She tol' me 'bout my paw and how he had fell off a bluff in Memphis and stuck a sharp rock right through his head. They tuk him back to the plantation and wropped him in a blanket and buried him. That was all I ever knowed 'bout him.[19]

Her father's death was apparently accidental, but clearly her mother was brutally treated as a slave and suffered a severe head injury as a consequence of resisting a whipping. It is evident that while she was a slave, Redmoun had little access to information about her family. Redmoun's mistress protected her from physical punishment but found other means to punish her:

> I had good times when I was little girl. I jest played 'round the place and got into devilment. Sometimes Mr. Scruggs would say, "I'm gonna' whup that brat." Miss Gusta would say, "No you ain't goin' lay yo' hans on her an iffen you do, I'm goin' quit you." Miss Gusta was indifferent in quality from Mr. Scruggs. He fooled her to marry him, lettin' on like he got lot of things he ain't got. . . .
>
> Miss Gusta never did hit me in her life but she punished

me terrible. She get the Bible and read me 'bout my sins
and put me in the black dark closet to steddy 'bout my sins
'til I could ask God's forgiveness and come to her and tell
her that I was sorry. I studied over my sins so much I 'cided
I was through with sinning.[20]

It is interesting to note the way in which Redmoun rates the
quality of whites on the basis of their treatment of slaves. Her
empirical definition of the problem of slavery is expressed in
terms of particular cases and experiences. However, in general
she does not condemn or condone the institution of slavery.

As expected, the four ex-slaves offer differing definitions of
the problem of slavery based on personal experience and other
empirical evidence. Franks and Little remember slavery as a
good system that worked to their own personal benefit and to
the benefit of others; Kelly evaluates slavery as an evil system
that worked to the economic benefit of whites at the expense of
blacks; and Redmoun, who was oblivious to her slave status prior
to her emancipation, assesses slavery as good for some slaves
and bad for others. With the exception of Kelly, they tend to
view the peculiar race relations associated with the institution
of slavery in positive terms and willingly identify with the "quality" and benevolence of their former owners. Kelly acknowledges that her mistress was good in comparison with other
whites, but characterizes the race relations of slavery as enmity
between whites and blacks. Slavery is understood by these ex-
slaves to be a system of reciprocal obligations between owner
and slave, but all four tend to base their empirical definitions
of the situation on the practical question of humane treatment
rather than on the perception that the system was inherently
right or wrong.

AFFIRMATIONS OF LOYALTY

According to Potter, the affirmation of loyalty involves the
creation of "expressive symbols which represent a center of
value, locus of commitment, or source of identity."[21] Although
the four ex-slaves have not self-consciously created or designated specific symbols for such a purpose, a careful reading
reveals that the characteristic forms of expression that they use

to describe themselves also convey value, commitment, and identity. The expressive symbol that emerges in Franks's narrative is "pet," which is also his given name. For Kelly, the expressive symbol is "sister," a title that bears religious significance. Little identifies with the expressive symbol "ole southern(er)." Redmoun's expressive symbol comes forth in her description of herself as a "present" to white folks. These four symbols—pet, sister, ole southerner, and present—provide a convenient frame of reference for analyzing affirmations of loyalty with a view toward illuminating the center of value, locus of commitment, and source of identity that underlie the ethical perspective of each of the four informants with regard to the problem of slavery.

A *pet* is an animal kept for amusement or companionship, or a person especially loved or indulged.[22] It is evident from the interviews of both Pet Franks and his wife, Dora Franks, that Pet was his given name and not a nickname. However, Pet Franks sees himself playing the role of a pet in relation to whites, both in slavery and in freedom. With pride he declares his continuing ties with whites: "Fact is I'se worked right round white folks most all my days."[23] Franks served his former master as a house servant, as a field hand, and as a valet during the Civil War. Moreover, he served the Confederate troops as a waiter and nurse. After the war he claims to have supported the political interests of the local whites by organizing blacks to vote the Democratic ticket:

> After de war de Yankees, dey called demselves Publicans den, dey come down here and wanted all de niggers to vote de Publican ticket. Den, lemme tell you, I went to work for my white folks down here. Dey was holdin' big meetin's and speakin's but I was workin' too and on 'lection day I brung in 1500 niggers to vote de Democrat ticket. De folks what saw us comin' over de hill say we look like big black cloud, and I reckon we sounded like one too with all our hollerin' and shoutin'.[24]

It can be assumed that Franks was encouraged and aided by his white folks in his efforts to organize black voters en masse to preserve the political interests of local whites. His ingratiating attitude and self-serving behavior seem to have played a part in alienating him from other blacks, including his own wife and children. Franks claims that he moved to the country to be near the white patrons of the fishing lodge and to get away from the blacks in the town. Yet he evokes negative racial stereotypes to condemn other blacks in order to justify his own isolation:

> They ain't got no sense now days. All dey believes in now is drinkin' and carousin'. Dey ain't got no use for nothin' but a little corn likker and a good fight! I doan believe in no such gwinens on, no sir ree. Dat's de reason I stays out here by myself all de time. I doan want to have nothin' to do with dem. I goes to town 'bout once a month to get s'pplies but I doan never fool round wid dem niggers den. I gets 'long wid my white folks tho'. All de mens and womens what comes out here to de club is powerful good to me.[25]

Not only does the stereotypical representation of carousing blacks serve to justify Franks's self-imposed exile, but it also sets him apart from the "bad niggers" who in freedom have forsaken the servile posture of slaves and have forfeited the favor and indulgence of whites. Franks's statement suggests that he has made a conscious decision to court the favor and support of whites at the cost of living apart from the black community in town. However, his isolation is not absolute and entire. When the interviewer asks if he gets lonesome in the country, Franks admits enjoying the company of a black female neighbor on occasion:

> Me get lonesome? Lawdee no mam! I has my two dogs and den white folks is allus comin' out here an dey is good to me. Aint I got no colored neighbors? Yes mam, dere is one right peart nigger woman what lives down de road a piece. Her name is Katie and I goes down dere every once in a while when I gets tired of eatin' my own cookin' and she sets a plum good table.[26]

Pet also says that he goes into town to visit his wife, Dora, once a month. (Dora was interviewed by the same interviewer, Mrs. Richard Kolb.) It is interesting to note how her attitudes toward blacks and whites differ from his, despite the fact that, like Pet, she confesses to be a Christian and claims to have experienced good treatment as a slave:

> Lawd, yes, Miss, dese here young folks today is gwine straight to de Devil. All dey do all day and all night is run around and drink corn likker and ride automobiles. I'se got a grandaughter here dat's as wild as de rest of dem and I worries right smart 'bout her, but it doan do no good case her mammy let her do jest as she please anyway. Den I tells you de one thing I worries most about and dat is de white folks what lives here midst de niggers. You knows what kinda folks dey is and it sho is bad influence on dem. You knows niggers ain't supposed to allus know de right from de wrong case dey ain't allus been taught but for de white folks to come down here and do lak dey do, I tells you, it aint right. De good white folks oughter do somethin' 'bout it. You is heared of dis Miss Sally what lives out here? She lays wid de men all day and all night and de chillen hangs round and peeps thru de winder at her goin's on and laughs at her an think they is smart. Now you know dat ain't no way to raise chillen up. Dey larns all dat devilment soon enough 'thout a white woman settin' such a bad 'zample for dem. Why when I was a kid dey allus told me dat babies was found in stumps and I believed dat until I was grown and went 'round lookin' in every stump I see a trying' to find a baby for me and Miss Emmaline. I was right smart disappointed when I found out better.
>
> Dem was purty good days way back yonder during slavery times anyways. 'Cose I don't believe in slavery case it aint in de Bible and I is a good Christian.[27]

Instead of glorifying her pleasant memories of slavery, Dora rejects slavery based on her understanding of the Bible and the Christian faith. She condemns the behavior of the current generation of blacks, which she attributes to their lack of moral training and the poor example being set by whites.

At any rate, for Pet Franks the cost of being a pet is to live in a state of relative isolation and alienation in exchange for the benefit of steady employment. His center of value is survival, his locus of commitment is white patronage, and his source of identity is his slave past. Although he describes himself as one who has got religion, his conversion experience does not seem to have any ongoing significance beyond his baptism. His values, commitment, and identity, as conveyed by the symbolic status of being a pet, are devoid of any references to God or religious faith.

Sister Kelly took on the title of *Sister* as a consequence of her conversion: "I never will forget that morning when I was saved by his blood, and changed to the woman you see today. I'm sho' Sister Kelly now."[28] The title Sister confers religious status. There are evangelical and holiness churches where all believers are addressed as Brother and Sister, but Kelly assumes her title without making any mention of a church (except for a passing reference to clandestine slave prayer meetings). She refers to herself as Sister Kelly throughout the narrative, and at no point does she reveal her given name. It is clear that she perceives her status of Sister as having been established on the basis of her relationship with God. Her primary concern throughout the interview is to explain her conversion experience as an initiation into a life of piety and to share her knowledge of God with her interviewers. Her past impressions of slavery are negative, but slavery is important to her only insofar as it is the setting in which her conversion occurred. During the course of her interview, she seems to be somewhat annoyed by the fact that her interviewers are more interested in her slave experience than in her conversion experience:

Honey, right now you young folks is blind, deaf and dumb to the knowledge of God's name; that can't last, you gonna change, do you hear me? We can't do no good unless we got God in our heart, and our heads too. Bless God, he holds you in the hollow of his hand, and when he changes yo' soul, you gonna make the world know it, do you hear me? You young folks can't carry on yo' wicked ways without some kinda terrible fall, do you hear me: I ain't carring nothin' 'bout nothing else but God now. He's got me in the hollow of his most holy hand. You youngsters don't understand that, but you mark my word, you will 'fore it's done with. You young folks don't want to humble youself to the Lord and ask him for these things, but I'm going home to Jesus, yessir, oooh praise His holy name. . . .

Well, you young folks wants to know all 'bout everything but the Lord; now you wants to know 'bout cures for rheumatism. Well, people used to get polk root, and sasaparilla for rheumatism.[29]

Kelly's preaching reveals that her center of value is her knowledge of God, her locus of commitment is her heavenly home, and her source of identity is her conversion experience. She gained access to knowledge of God by hearing God's voice, by being touched by God's Spirit, and by learning how to pray with God's words:

Yessir, I heard him all in the inside, saying "Come unto me, oh my little one, what makes you so hard to believe when you know I am the one and only God, and there ain't but one God but me?" Seems jest like yesterday 'stid of years and years ago, and I still feels the blessed spirit jest like brand new. . . .

Well, I still didn't know nothin' 'bout praying, but I says "Oooh, my good and holy Father, what can I say to Thee for Thy blessings," and he said in a voice that shook me like a storm, "Open your mouth and I will fill it with all the elements from on high.". . .

I tell you, honey, you got to be touched from the inside, and be struck by his hand like I was 'fore you feel that holy uplifting spirit.

Well, the last time the Lord spoke to me, he said, "My little one, I have carried you out of this world, and you is no more of this world, but of another world, the holy world, and they will hate you for my sake." That's the truth, ain't it. I don't fear no man but Jesus. He is my God, do you hear me?[30]

Thus Kelly affirms that her loyalty belongs exclusively to God. She mentions that she was married to Jim Kelly, and that she had three children at the beginning of the Civil War, but she does not discuss her marital and parental relationships in terms of loyalty. Her values, commitment, and identity all derive from her relationship with God, not from ties to family, church, whites, or other blacks. Her center of value is what God requires of her, her locus of commitment is the heavenly reward God has promised to provide, and her identity is determined by the experience of being changed by the power of God. From this vantage point she regards slavery as a temporary evil God enabled her to endure and overcome. Thus, she has no continuing obligations of loyalty to the values and relationships of her slave past. It is apparent that even while she was in bondage, her self-image was shaped by her conversion experience and not by her slave status.

Wesley Little identifies closely with the "ole southern(er)," who prospered in the "good ole days" of slavery. He speaks with pride of the successes of his master and other southern white farmers who relied upon slave labor to build their fortunes. Little claims to have been treated well in bondage. Because his farm was small (thirty-five or forty acres), Little's master did the overseeing and whipping himself. Some of Little's strongest affirmations of loyalty stem from his childhood memories of the moral instruction, and whippings, he received from his master:

> I wuz a slave 'till I wuz 'bout nineteen years ole an' I can truthfully say I never got but two whippin's from my Marse de whole time an' dey wuz when I wuz a little chap, an' I'll thank him 'till my dying day fer dem thrashin's fer I deserved both ob 'em an' dey helped to shape de straight, honest life I'se lived. One whippin' wuz 'bout de middle o' de day. I wuz helpin' Marse in de lot, he wanted to tie a ox to a post an' he sont me to de house fer some rope dat wuz in de pantry. I didn't hab on no pants jes' a long shirt. Aunt Hetty, de cook had jes' turnt out some o' de bes' lookin' egg bread. I went to de table an' slipped a big piece under my shirt. I went on to de lot an' handed Marse de rope an' den he spied dat I had some 'em hid under my shirt. He ask me whut it wuz an' I tole him I didn't

hab nothing hid under my shirt. He didn't even look to see whut I had hid. He got a keen switch an' give me a good thrashin'. When I quieted off he called me to him an' give me a good talk. He say he didn't whip me 'cause ob de bread but fer tellin' a lie an' de talk he give me dat mornin' 'bout bein' honest an' truthful has stuck wid me all dese years. Den de nex' whippin' I got wuz 'bout bein' careless an' lettin' some cattle get out, an' by gittin' (out) dey done a heap o' damage. Marse tole me dat time dat it warn't de loss I cause him dat he whipped me fer, it wuz fer not bein' trustworthy. He made me set down in de shade ob a big tree by de ole pasture gate an' give me another talk an' from dat good day I ain't never willfully betrayed another trust.[31]

Little expresses gratitude for these whippings because they taught him the importance of being truthful and trustworthy. Moreover, he offers proof of how well he learned these moral lessons with an illustration of his loyalty to the task of protecting his master's children:

An' time after time Marse has sont me wid his little girls on des fo' mile walk to Church. He knowed dey wuz safe wid me, he knowed I'd a fought like a tiger to have protected one ob 'em.[32]

It is obvious why a slave master would value virtues such as these in a servant, but it is curious to observe how a former slave would extol his own virtues in this regard. The interviewer, Mrs. D. W. Giles, makes note of the fact that Little has a "reputation for unquestionable integrity," which she illustrates with a story of how he worked for years to repay a debt to the widow of a man to whom he owed five hundred dollars, in spite of the fact that the widow disavowed all knowledge of Little's indebtedness to her late husband.[33] Little speaks of how he raised his children to be Christians, implying that he passed on to them the same moral and religious training that he had received as a child from his master and mistress. It should be noted that Little's loyalty to his former owners seemed to come to an abrupt end after freedom, because he left with his "folks" to settle on a little farm. If his allegiance to his former owners is strictly a matter of nostalgic recollections, his ties to family have ongoing significance for him both in the past and in the present. In any case, it can be concluded that Little's center of value is a model of moral integrity that extols the virtues of truth-telling and trustworthiness. His locus of commitment is the Old South, here envisioned as an ethos which sustained positive moral and religious influences. He calls himself a "good Christian," therefore his source of identity, generally speaking, is the Christian religion.

Although he gives an account of his childhood conversion, and says that he preached for twenty years, it is significant that he does not relate this morality to religion in a direct way. However, morality and religion are much more important than race as determinants of his sense of self and social relations. He speaks of blacks, both in slavery and in freedom, using derogatory stereotypes (as happy coons, or as smart and hard-headed freed niggers). Yet the point of his discussion seems to be to depict the Old South as a bygone era of good race relations that instilled moral virtues which outlived the institution of slavery. The only critical perspectives Little offers (without comment or explanation) regarding the ethics of slavery are his account of his father's escape to fight for the Yankees, and his statement that at the end of the war "de slaves wuz turnt loose wid no way to take care o' dem selves."[34] Little makes a curious acknowledgment of the dubious tone of his happy recollections of slavery: "Dis may not sound lak slaves days but I had a good master that sho' 'nuf looked after us in de right way."[35]

Laura Redmoun, having been given to her old mistress's daughter for a wedding present at the age of 6 months, describes herself as a "present" to the white folks. Being a present to whites meant that, for the most part, she lived in isolation from her family and other blacks. Redmoun recalls that as a child she was unaware of the fact that she was a slave and black:

> Law, I didn't know I was no slave. I thought I was white and plumb indifferent from the Niggers. I was right

'sprised when I found out I was Nigger just like the other black faces.[36]

As has been noted previously, even when emancipation came and she was informed by her mistress that she was no longer a slave, Redmoun still claimed ignorance of her slave status. Redmoun seems to have experienced slavery in a passive way. Her remembrances of slavery are devoid of any reference to work; she experienced slavery more as a surrogate child than as a servant. Evidently her role as a "present" afforded her the luxury of being naive and irresponsible. Because her mistress protected her (from physical abuse) from infancy until the age of 17 (when she was given in marriage from her mistress's deathbed), Redmoun tends to remember her mistress as a parent figure. However, the loyalty she gave to her mistress was not applied to other whites, as illustrated by the fact that she relied upon her mistress to protect her from being punished by her mistress's husband whenever he grew intolerant of Redmoun's behavior. Moreover, Redmoun draws a clear class distinction between her mistress and her mistress's husband, whom she never refers to as her master:

Miss Gusta was indifferent in quality from Mr. Scruggs. He fooled her to marry him, lettin' on like he got a lot of things he ain't got. ... He was a curious kind of man it 'pears to me iffen I'm to tell the plain out truth. I don't think he was much but kinda trashy.[37]

As an adult, Redmoun did acknowledge and value her family and marital bonds, both in the case of her mother, with whom she was reunited after slavery, and her husband, whom she remembers as a good man and a good worker. She continued to work for whites after she was married, but does not show any particular loyalty or affinity to whites outside the context of her experience in slavery. Redmoun's center of value appears to be survival, interpreted here as freedom from abuse. She especially values the fact that she was never abused in slavery or in freedom. It is solely on the basis of the presence or absence of abuse that she evaluates the institution of slavery in ethical terms—it was not a bad experience for her personally because she was not abused, but it was a horrible experience for her mother, who incurred assaults both to her body and to her human dignity in slavery. It is difficult to discern the contours of Redmoun's locus of commitment; during slavery, she was totally committed to her mistress, but after freedom her family became her central concern. In her introductory comments, interviewer Heloise M. Foreman states that "Laura terms herself a whitefolk's Nigger."[38] However, because no such statement appears in the text of the interview, it will be assumed that, when speaking for herself, Redmoun did not affirm her loyalties to whites on this level and in this manner. The few references Redmoun makes to whites in tracing the course of her life after slavery are made in the context of employment and not as declarations of loyalty, admiration, or affection. In view of the fact that she discusses her childhood conversion experience in explicit detail and concludes her interview with a description of herself as a good Christian and a good person, perhaps it is fair to conclude that her source of identity ultimately lies in her Christian faith and not in her initial description of herself as a present to white folks.

MODES OF ETHICAL REASONING

In *Getting Saved from the Sixties: Moral Meaning in Conversion and Cultural Change*, Steven M. Tipton formulates a taxonomy of four styles of ethical evaluation, building upon Potter's paradigm of the ethical system: 1) the authoritative style, oriented toward an authoritative moral source known by faith; 2) the regular style, oriented toward rules or principles known by reason; 3) the consequential style, oriented toward consequences known by cost-benefit calculation; and 4) the expressive style, oriented toward the quality of personal feelings and of situations known by intuition.[39]

In describing their own practical moral responses to the problem of slavery as slaves who were also confessing Christians, the four ex-slaves employ modes of ethical reasoning that resemble the alternative forms of discourse identified by Tipton. Sister Kelly has adopted an authoritative ethical style and form of discourse; the style and discourse of Wesley Little could be clas-

sified as regular; Pet Franks, consequential; and Laura Redmoun, expressive.

The authoritative style and mode of ethical discourse is
ascribed to individuals who are concerned to respond morally
to a situation first by relying upon faith to ascertain what God
has commanded, and then by obeying God's revealed require-
ments. In her conversion experience, Kelly is initiated into an
intimate relationship with God, who speaks directly to her and
manifests divine power and guidance to her in other ways. During the course of her discussion of the injustices perpetrated by
slave-holding whites, she affirms that knowing God was the only
effective way of coping with the problem of slavery:

> I tell you, honey, I wuked and lived with good ones and
> bad ones, too. You got to know something 'bout the Lord
> to git along anywhere. You don't know nothin' 'bout him?
> Well, you better know him; better learn 'bout him, that's
> what'll help you.[40]

Both the tone and content of her moral discourse reflect an
authoritative orientation; obviously Kelly is trying to persuade
her interviewer to embrace her religion by demonstrating how
it helped her to survive slavery and by asserting that knowledge
of God is necessary and sufficient for dealing with any difficulties
encountered in life. Her grasp of what God commands and her
desire to be obedient and faithful are based on her recurrent
experiences of direct revelation—God guides, protects, and
speaks to her as she listens and prays. Moreover, her knowledge
of God is bolstered by her understanding of the Bible. Although
she admits that she can neither read nor write, she claims to
have learned the Bible by rote. She does not condemn slavery
on the basis of what God has commanded, but rather on account
of the suffering and inequities it produced. She recalls partici-
pating in clandestine slave prayer meetings. Prayer is the only
recourse for the deliverance of the slave—it is seen as the only
effective response to the problem of slavery. More important,
the ability to pray has a much greater significance than the desire
for release from bondage; when she came to know God and
received the words of prayer from the Spirit of God, her ethical

orientation shifted from the affairs of the present world and its troubles to a longing for the next world and its rewards. Slavery is one of many evil circumstances encountered in her life where God exercised the power of deliverance. Being obedient and faithful to God seems to be her overriding ethical concern.

The regular style and mode of ethical discourse seek to conform to the relevant rule or principle in confronting a moral dilemma. Wesley Little learned well the lessons of the slave master's whip and moral instruction. Integrity, truthfulness, and trustworthiness are upheld by him both as a slave and as a free man, especially with regard to financial obligations. Little's Christian conversion occurs in response to the sermon of a white preacher in a "white folks meeting house" with segregated seating for slaves, and he relies upon his mistress for spiritual guidance once he decides that he should join the church. Yet Little's moral training is not a matter of religious faith and conviction; rather, it is the consequence of being trained and disciplined by his master in the virtues that make a good slave. Little internalizes these virtues and passes them on to his children. In his old age he rejoices in the "straight, honest life" he has lived in adherence to the rules and principles he was taught. He has a very clear sense of what is right or obligatory according to the rules; in his view the institution of slavery was morally correct insofar as truthfulness, trustworthiness, and other moral virtues were upheld by slave and master.

The focus of the consequential style and mode of ethical discourse is to define and pursue one's wants. Pet Franks exemplifies this category of moral reasoning as an individual who willingly isolates himself physically and psychologically from other blacks so as to make himself secure financially in the service of whites. He acknowledges that some slaves were cruelly treated, but seems to regard such cases as exceptions to the rule. Slavery was good in that it afforded him the opportunity to live and work in close proximity with whites who wielded economic and political power. He enjoyed being a general-purpose slave to good white folks; he served soldiers in the Confederate Army during the Civil War, and he organized blacks to vote for Southern Democrats during Reconstruction. Eventually Franks left his wife and family to move to the country and work as a cook in a fishing lodge with a white clientele. His condemnation of other blacks is also based on a calculation of consequences; he sees an advantage in distancing himself from their carousing and disorderly behavior. Franks's lifestyle and ideas are effective in producing the desired benefits from whites; the cost is alienation from other blacks, including his own family.

The expressive style and mode of ethical discourse lead the individual to respond to what is happening with the act that best fits the situation at hand. Laura Redmoun exhibits this ethical style. She does not appeal to divine moral authority or to moral rules and principles; she does not weigh the costs and benefits of a particular course of moral action in light of her own wants. She merely reacts and responds morally according to her feelings and perceptions. She cannot condemn slavery based on her personal experience because she grew up not knowing that she was in bondage. The serious injury that her mother suffered as a slave only leads her to deplore the brutality of the whites who beat her, not the injustice of an institution that allows cruel, punitive measures. When the Union forces invaded Memphis in an assault that eventually led to her emancipation, she reacted in fear, her primary concern being to protect her mistress's valuables from plunder. Being free did not mean anything to her, because at the moment her frame of mind was expressive of an appreciation of survival and security. It is important for her to be able to say that she had never been abused in her life. Even in the course of her conversion account, Redmoun is careful to note that the dress she "slapped the sides out of" in her religious ecstasy was a good dress made of percale, a higher quality of fabric than was worn by other slaves.[41] Thus Redmoun's moral discourse on slavery centers on her feelings about how she and others were treated as individuals, not on any particular norms or consequences related to the ethics of the institution itself. She concludes that she has no complaints to make but, hard times notwithstanding, has been able to maintain herself by working and by being a good person and a good Christian.

Quasi-Theological

The fourth and final analytical category of Potter's paradigm is quasi-theological beliefs concerning God, humankind, and human destiny. Potter ascribes particular importance to "anthropological assumptions concerning the range of human freedom and man's power to predict and control historical events."[42] Thus this fourth analytical category seems especially appropriate for exploring the quasi-theological beliefs of Christian slaves with regard to the idea of freedom.

Only two of the four respondents speak of God in their interviews: Kelly and Redmoun. Kelly offers a thoroughgoing description of her understanding of God. Beginning with her conversion experience, she explains the progressive revelations she received concerning the nature and power of God. Her belief is that there is one and only one God, who is addressed by her as Father, manifested to her as Jesus, and felt in her as Spirit. God's attributes include goodness, holiness, justice, and might. The dominant anthropomorphic image in her statement is that of God's hand; when converted she was "struck by his hand," in adversity she "held on to His blessed hand," and now she finds refuge "in the hollow of his most holy hand." God's hand administers power and grace to change the human soul by means of conversion. Praise and prayer are regarded as the proper religious responses to God's providential care and protection, and God even supplies the words of prayer and blessing.[43]

Redmoun, in keeping with her expressive ethical style, only speaks of God in the context of her ecstatic religious experience. Prior to her conversion, "the Lord got to working' right inside" her as she listened to the sermons preached at her mistress's church. Next, her mistress imposed upon her, as an act of discipline, a requirement to seek God's forgiveness. Finally, the "glory of God jest 'cended right down" on her, and for three days she wandered through a remote area shouting "I got Jesus." All of her references to God express the notion of possession; she begins by receiving certain distinctive religious sensations, and ultimately she declares that she possesses God. God's only attribute seems to be a glory that is manifested in her as ecstasy.[44]

It is significant that both Kelly and Redmoun describe God primarily with reference to religious experience. Although Kelly states that slaves on the auction block prayed to God for deliverance, neither she nor Redmoun interprets the experience of emancipation in theological terms. It is even more significant that Franks and Little eliminate all talk of God from their stories, perhaps out of a reluctance to enlist God in their defense of slavery and good white slave holders.

The four respondents show more of a consensus in their beliefs concerning humankind and human destiny. All tend to categorize people in terms of race, social status, and morality. Franks is careful to describe his former owner and overseer, as well as his present benefactors, as good white folks. Little remembers his former master and mistress as being good. Even Kelly, who is critical of the institution of slavery, gives a qualified description of her former mistress as "good as most any old white woman." Redmoun does not explicitly use the term "good" in describing her former mistress, but she does so implicitly by expressing the opinion that her mistress's husband was "kind of trashy" by comparison. Redmoun believes that in general there are two kinds of people in the world, the good ones and the mean ones, and she identifies with the good ones.

The four ex-slaves' assumptions concerning the "range of human freedom and man's power to predict and control historical events" vary greatly. For Franks, freedom means isolation from other blacks and contact with patronizing whites. Kelly's freedom is defined and ordered for her by God, its material and social contours being obscured by her vision of eternal salvation. Little's concept of freedom consists in the possibility of enjoying a "smooth and quiet" life in conformity with the virtues of truthfulness, trustworthiness, and moral integrity. For Redmoun, freedom is a testimony of not having ever been physically abused. What all four hold in common, however, is the experience of having made the transition from slavery to freedom, not by their own action, but in the course of history. As former slaves, they assess the ability of men and women to predict and control historical events in terms of their direct experience of the power of one racial group to hold another in bondage.

SUMMARY

To summarize the ethical perspectives of the four ex-slaves with respect to slavery, Franks and Little view slavery as good,

Kelly views it as evil, and Redmoun is ambivalent. It is evident that their ethical perspectives correlate rather closely with their evaluation of treatment; it already has been demonstrated that their empirical definitions of the situation are based primarily on the practical criterion of treatment.

From the four ethical statements emerge two basic patterns of response to the question of what moral realignments and ethical perspectives were created in the lives of the slaves as a consequence of the experience of conversion: the convert either condemns slavery, or the convert makes no ethical assessment at all of slavery, seeing slavery and conversion as independent experiences.

Sister Kelly sees slavery and conversion as conflicting ideals; she had a negative experience of slavery and an intensely positive experience of conversion. Conversion gave her a new center of value, locus of commitment, and source of identity, which she, together with other slaves, brought to bear upon her condition of bondage by means of prayers for deliverance. God is the authoritative source of her personal morality and her social ethics, notwithstanding her belief that God has called her to give up on the world and affirm her loyalty to heaven.

Pet Franks evaluated slavery in positive terms, but his conversion seems to be a past memory of momentary ecstasy with little ongoing significance in his moral life. His consequentialist ethics addresses the relation between the ethical ideals of slavery and conversion by subverting the concerns of both to the end of economic security. In other words, Franks is more conscientious about playing the roles defined for him by whites during slavery than he is about being guided and informed by Christian teaching. He does not describe himself as a good Christian.

Wesley Little claims to have had a comfortable existence as a slave and a meaningful childhood conversion experience. His religious experience led to his being called to preach, which he did for twenty years. However, Little's normative ethics, having been instituted by his master's whip, seems unrelated to his religious experience. His "straight and honest life" is the result of his adherence, both in slavery and in freedom, to those virtues especially valued in a good servant—truthfulness and trustworthiness. Little sees himself as a good Christian, but he appeals to his moral integrity as a vindication of his slave experience.

Finally, Laura Redmoun, a "present" to white folks from birth, evaluates both her conversion experience and her slave experience strictly in terms of feelings and response. She denies ever knowing that she was a slave, but she very clearly recalls having had an ecstatic conversion experience when she "got Jesus." Her ethical perspectives on slavery and conversion can be regarded as independent in the sense that she seems to have adopted an expressive ethical style in everything, taking each life experience and encounter on its own terms. She calls herself a good Christian, but has doubts as to whether she ever really was a slave.

This sample of ex-slave Christians does not necessarily include any saints or heroes; rather, it is composed of ordinary people. Their narratives present a broad spectrum of slave life and treatment, conversion, experiences, theological convictions, and ethical perspectives. However, the analysis of their diversity along these lines reveals a critical point of consensus; namely, *none* of them *defends* slavery on the ground of Christian ethics. These former slaves do not posit a positive relationship between personal moral realignments brought about by the experience of conversion and social ethical endorsements of slavery engendered by the experiences of good treatment. None of them is ever actually converted to a white gospel of submission, even if they have consented to adopt the demeaning social roles whites imposed upon them. The candor of their remembrances of slavery, the integrity of their relationships with whites, their opinions on race relations in general, their use of derogatory stereotypes in describing other blacks, and any number of related factors may be viewed askance by modern observers. Yet, all of these ex-slaves take care to draw the lines of their religious testimony and their slave testimony so as to avoid voicing the conclusion that slavery is sanctioned and supported by the Christian faith. Even in the course of recalling their most ingenuous and nostalgic memories of the "good old days" of slavery under the "good white folks," they stop short of making the confession that either the past enslavement or the continuing subjugation of black people is in keeping with the will and the ways of God.

The conversion experience did not transform them into adherents of the slave ethic taught and upheld by their oppressors, even if it did make them "better" slaves by bringing an increased measure of moral integrity and conscientiousness into their lives and labors as slaves. If there is any social ethic at all among the ex-slave converts, it is indeed an ethic of liberation and not one of submission to the institution of slavery or to the bondage of oppressive religious beliefs and ideas.

OTHER ETHICAL RESPONSES TO SLAVERY

Certainly there were Christian slaves who openly condemned the institution of slavery on the ground of a Christian ethic of liberation. Pet Franks's wife, Dora, rejects slavery "case it aint in de Bible and I is a good Christian." Either Dora Franks is unaware of the passages of the Bible that deal with slavery or ignores them. Mary Colbert, an ex-slave who reports having been treated well as a slave, nevertheless attributes the demise of the institution of slavery to the will of God:

> Yes, Honey, I was raised and loved by my own white folks and, when I grew to be old enough and large enough, I worked for them. I have been with, or worked for, white folks all my life and, just let me tell you, I had the best white folks in the world, but it was by God's plan that the Negroes were set free.[45]

It is significant that Colbert's ethical assessment of slavery is made with reference to the will and plan of God and transcends the criterion of treatment. Miss Catherine, who also claims to have been treated well, signifies that the moral responses of well-treated slaves to the problem of slavery emerged as a matter of conscience: "They was happy in them days; only thing, they didn't feel right about was belonging to the white folks."[46] Jefferson Franklin Henry, a Baptist preacher and pastor, offers a retrospective ethical evaluation of slavery when asked to express his opinions concerning Abraham Lincoln, Jefferson Davis, and the comparison of slavery and freedom:

> Now that it's all been over more than 70 years and us is had time to study it over good, I thinks it was by God's

own plan that President Abraham Lincoln sot us free, and I can't sing his praises enough. Miss Martha named me for Jeff Davis, so I can't down him when I'se got his name; I was named for him and Benjamin Franklin too. Oh! Sho, I'd ruther be free and I believes the Negroes is got as much right to freedom as any other race, 'deed I does believe that.[47]

These responses serve to illustrate that there were Christian slaves whose social ethics regarding slavery were expressed as a matter of belief, albeit in many different ways. Dora Franks does not believe in slavery; Mary Colbert believes it was God's will for the slave to be set free, despite the benevolence of the best white folks; Miss Catherine's beliefs concerning slavery rest upon memories of a troubled conscience on the part of slaves who were well-treated but not free; and Reverend Henry's belief that blacks have as much right to freedom as whites is offered from the vantage point of studied retrospection of the facts of history in light of the plan of God.

Some of the former slaves condemned the institution of slavery on the basis of a social ethic that is more philosophical than theological in nature and took shape independently of their Christian convictions. These ethical critiques are usually offered in response to the question of whether slavery or freedom is better, or if slavery was "good" for blacks. The racist intentions of interviewers who pursue this line of questioning are often thinly veiled; there are attempts to force the ex-slaves to summarize their own life experiences with the admission that slavery was somehow better than freedom. However, the slaves' responses to these inquiries reveal their ability to answer honestly without angering or offending their white racist interviewers, and sometimes they communicated veiled messages of their own. Stephen McCray responds to a question concerning the benefits of slavery with a story that illustrates his position:

Every time I think of slavery and if it done the race any good, I think of the story of the coon and dog who met. The coon said to the dog "Why is it you're so fat and I am so poor, and we is both animals?" The dog said: "I lay round Master's house and let him kick me and he gives me a piece of bread right on." Said the coon to the dog: "Better then that I stay poor." Them's my sentiment. I'm lak the coon, I don't believe in 'buse.[48]

This story brings several key issues into focus, including inequities in the distribution of wealth, the question of racial equality, the meaning of freedom, submission to slavery as a matter of moral choice, and the immorality of abuse. He concludes that he does not believe in abuse, but there is no indication that this belief is based on religious faith. McCray's story suggests that the slaves actually debated the ethical dimensions of the problem of slavery among themselves.

Jack and Rosa Maddox, a married couple interviewed together in Dallas, Texas, express differing opinions with regard to the question of whether or not blacks were better off after slavery:

Yes I was born a slave and so was Rosa. We got out of the chattel slavery and I was better off for gettin' out but Rosa don't think so. She says all we freed for is to starve to death. I guess she's right 'bout that, too, for herself. She says her whitefolks were good to her. But don't you expect me to love my whitefolks. I love them like a dog loves hickory.

I was settin' here thinking the other night 'bout the talk of them kind of whitefolks going to Heaven. Lord God, they'd turn the Heaven wrong side out and have the angels working to make something they could take away from them. I can say these things now. I'd say them anywhere — in the courthouse — before the judges, before God.[49]

Jack's bitterness toward whites is attributable to the fact that he suffered many abuses and deprivations as a slave, and especially during his childhood, because his mother died when he was 3 or 4 years old. After emancipation he and Rosa were subject to further victimization, being cheated by whites when they attempted to purchase land and later while working as tenant farmers. Rosa was converted at a young age and was comparatively well-treated. Jack makes no claim to be a Christian. He scoffs at the idea of slave-holding whites going to heaven and is extremely critical of white preachers:

> Course we got to go to church in fair weather. They used to fix up a brush arbor in back of the whitefolks meeting house and let the niggers set out there. The white preacher would preach along and then he 'ud say, "And you slaves out there, if you want to have the Kingdom Come you got to mind your masters, work hard and don't steal your master's chickens."
>
> After I was a plumb old man I read in the papers that there was nine hundred preachers in the penitentiary and I said to myself, "There ought to be nine hundred more there if they would just ketch them all. Them preachers and their left-handed fellowship!"[50]

Jack's attitudes toward slavery differ from Rosa's due to the perception that emancipation brought less suffering for him, and more suffering for her, in comparison with slavery. He steadfastly refuses to "love" white folks, but his memories of a deprived childhood moved him to show compassion by adopting an abused child long after their own children were grown:

> Well when we was pretty old we knew a woman had a baby. She treated that baby pitiful bad. She said he looked like he was a idiot. I remembered 'bout how miserable I was when I was a little boy and I said to Rosa if she was willing we would take him. She was willing and the mother gave him to us when he was twenty-two months old. He was covered with sores but a little washing soon cleared it up and he's been with us every since like our boy. He is a smart nice boy. He is 'bout fifteen now.[51]

Thus both Jack and Rosa, married sixty-nine years at the time of their joint interview, display a loving sensitivity to black suffering, yet have radically different sentiments toward whites and the problem of slavery.

CONCLUSION

The point of this discussion has been to demonstrate the diversity of ethical thought concerning slavery that is represented among those who experienced both slavery and conversion. To be sure, there were slaves who developed a liberation ethic on the ground of Christian faith. Moreover, there is little evidence that any of the slaves accepted the white racist ethic of submission that was presented to them, or the theological argument that it was the will of God for them to suffer as slaves. While some ex-slaves apparently had no social ethic at all with regard to slavery, or none that they were willing to share with their white interviewers, they still tended to resist endorsing the institution of slavery on theological or ethical grounds. And even in cases where an individual had no personal experience of abusive treatment in slavery, there was a tendency to take seriously the suffering of other slaves as a point of departure for challenging the morality of the slave system. Without question, the experience of conversion did generate a liberation ethic among the slaves, but such an ethic was not universally articulated in the ex-slave oral histories. Significantly, some of the most powerful ethical claims against slavery made by ex-slaves have their foundation in a personal affirmation of God's love as experienced in religious conversion and practice, and in the confidence that God has fully authorized them to risk the danger of speaking boldly of liberation in an oppressive milieu.

SLAVE NARRATIVES, BLACK THEOLOGY OF LIBERATION (USA), AND THE FUTURE

George C. L. Cummings

Contemporary black theology (USA) emerged in the late 1960s in order to confront the ideological role of racism and white supremacy in the theological views and practices of the North American Christian community and to establish the theological foundations for the development of a theology grounded in the experiences of the black oppressed community in the United States.[1] The basic problem being addressed was, according to Gayraud Wilmore, "A culture which equated the authority and omnipotence of Euro-American white men with the authority and omnipotence of God Himself [sic], a culture which for almost two thousand years created deity in the image of the white man and gave to God the attributes of Caucasian idealization."[2] Prominent in Wilmore's analysis of the function of black theology was the need to ground black theological discourse in black religious and cultural sources and to "return to the religious genius of the ancestors who came from places other than Europe."[3]

This collection of essays shares a common view that the slave narratives are a legitimate source of the experiences of black

oppressed people in the USA, as well as of the theological interpretations of their experiences of enslavement. Concomitantly,
the slave narratives provide a means to return to the religious
genius of the ancestors, who were forcibly taken from Africa
and made to serve in the brutal crucible of chattel slavery. The
narratives provide us with insight concerning the religious and
cultural world-views that informed black slaves' theological
interpretation of their experience and can be the basis upon
which contemporary black theologians can incorporate the "thematic universe" of the black oppressed into their discourse.[4]

These essays are an attempt to recover the theological images
and visions that were conditioned by the meaning-world of black
North American slaves and that they themselves utilized to
interpret their experiences of exploitation, suffering, and hope.
In methodological terms, then, this project presupposes an a
priori commitment to the thematic world of the black oppressed
and their struggles to transform their circumstances; it views the
slave narratives as a means of entering into the pre-textual world
of black oppressed people in order to derive images, values, and
symbols that might be useful in constructing a contemporary
black theology of liberation. By discerning the active and
dynamic presence of the Spirit in the midst of the slave experience, contemporary black theologians will discover the resources for a theological perspective that will empower the black
liberation struggle today.

The second conviction underlying this project flows from the
author's agreement with Sallie McFague that the abstract and
conceptual character of systematic theological discourse is too
remote from the kind of language that keeps faith and life
together. Thus it is necessary to develop a theological discourse
that can function as an intermediary between the language of
faith and life, and the language of systematic theology.[5]
McFague wishes to distinguish between classical models of systematic theology and doctrine that are dependent on the philosophical and often abstract language of the university, and the
discourse of life and faith and parabolic or metaphorical language that is "organically dependent on the metaphorical
base."[6] According to McFague, parabolic theory is derived from
the narrative traditions of a people and

finds that the genres most closely associated with it are the poem, the novel, and the autobiography, since these genres manifest the ways metaphor operates in language, belief, and life. Hence, they are prime resources for a theologian who is attempting an intermediary or parabolic theology — a theology that is, on the one hand, not itself parable and, on the other hand, not systematic theology, but a kind of theology which attempts to stay close to the parables.[7]

McFague call this *parabolic theology* because the language of metaphor is at the heart of all human experiences, of which the parable is the primary form of Christian discourse.[8] Accordingly, McFague contends, parabolic theology, grounded in the narratives of human experience, becomes a means whereby the theologian can derive generative themes in order to communicate in conceptual and linguistic terms that will empower and evoke the hearers to experience the Spirit through imaginative participation in the stories told. The evolution of a parabolic theological discourse rooted in the historical experiences and struggles of black slaves and derived from their narratives can provide us with a black theology that is empowering and transformative.

The third conviction that informs this project is our belief that the struggles of African American slaves amid the dialectic of despair and hope were the crucible for the creation of religio-cultural resources that sustained their lives and shaped their visions and hopes for a new and transformed future. The task of reconstructing a theological vision that will empower the contemporary struggle for black liberation will seek to utilize the resources created in the crucible of slavery.

The testimonies of the people, then, provide the basic raw data for the current project as black theologians continue to discover, within black religio-cultural sources, the material for a counter-hegemonic theological perspective. The purpose of this chapter is to identify some key issues that characterize the task of utilizing the slave narratives as a source for a black theology of liberation and to explicate the significance of the slave narrative perspective for black theology and worship, black theology and God, and a black liberation ethic.

SLAVE NARRATIVES, BLACK THEOLOGY, AND BLACK RELIGION

The diversity and complexity of the testimonies in the slave narratives are a witness to the complexity of any attempt to interpret their meaning theologically. First, the testimonies to the power of the Spirit in the slave community are themselves ambiguous in relationship to the specifically Christian content of those experiences. This intuition only confirms the point of view articulated by Gayraud Wilmore, for example, that the content of the religious experiences of African American slaves was only more or less Christian.[9]

In Chapter 3 Will Coleman also insists that the Spirit to which the slaves bear witness is only a "more or less Christian phenomenon," and he asserts that black theology should acknowledge this reality. As an interpreter of the slave narratives, Coleman is concerned that the narratives be allowed to be the vehicle of communicating the religious experiences of black slaves, and he challenges black theologians not to ignore "the diversity and totality of African American slaves' religious experiences . . . while attempting to build a theology based on their testimonies." His interest is in allowing the interpreter (himself) to be exposed to the symbolic-poetic world of the text as a means of allowing the text to be a means of engaging the interpreter in the reality to which it bears witness. Coleman cautions black theologians about their quick imposition of Christian categories upon the testimonies, but nevertheless continues by acknowledging that the mythopoetic world of the "slaves can enhance the praxis of liberation on the hermeneutical, linguistic-poetic front as well as in the political, social, economic struggles for full humanity."

The perspective that Will Coleman represents is one that both Dwight Hopkins and George C. L. Cummings acknowledge as being complementary to their own. In Chapter 1 Dwight Hopkins asserts that in the narratives "black bondsmen and bondswomen combined remnants of their African traditional religions with the justice message of the Christian gospel and planted the seeds for a black theology expressed through politics and culture." Hopkins and Cummings both acknowledge the diversity of witnesses in the slave narratives, but nevertheless contend that the task of interpretation is a complex one in which the interpreter is always involved as an interested partner.

Cummings has noted that the descriptive and interpretive moments of the hermeneutical task are inseparably interwoven. Thus, while he acknowledges Coleman's caution to allow the texts to speak for themselves, he is equally concerned that this complex task is one that presupposes an involved partner, the black theologian, whose a priori commitment to the black oppressed has been shaped by the gospel. The theological interpretation, then, emerges on the basis of the fact that the black theologian approaches these texts with the presupposition that the narratives contain the symbols, sensibilities, and values that constituted the basic materials of the religio-cultural world-views that black slaves constructed and which conditioned their hopes for a different and transformed future. The slave narratives give ample testimony to the genius of African American slaves, who combined the traditional African religions and Christianity into a religio-cultural resource that transformed their brute cultural encounters with raw and meaningless suffering into an experience of hope. However, unlike Coleman and Hopkins, Cummings is prepared to risk the identification of Jesus Christ—the paradigmatic manifestation of the God of liberation of crucifixion—with the presence of hope and the yearning for freedom in the black oppressed community. He is willing to acknowledge that his perspective is defined by an a priori commitment to the Christian perspective and to the black oppressed. It is black Christian theologians who engage in the task of explicating the meaning of the gospel from the perspective of the experiences of black oppressed people, and who intend to proceed upon the basis of this assumption while at the same time acknowledging the significance of Coleman's challenge.

In sum, then, while Coleman, Hopkins, and Cummings develop distinctive emphases and nuances in their particular projects, they have a common interest in acknowledging that insofar as contemporary black theology seeks to be faithful to the slave narratives and the gospel, then black theology must establish a methodological framework that both recognizes the "more or less Christian" character of the testimonies, while at the same time identifying specific theological criteria that establish linkage between their experiences of the Spirit and the paradigmatic revelation of God in Jesus as the Oppressed One.

Specifically, this common commitment means that black theologians must continue to devise a hermeneutical methodology that can incorporate both Christian and non-Christian paradigms in its discourse.

Another aspect of the complexity, and diversity, of slave testimonies is highlighted in Cheryl Sanders's contribution to this project. Sanders demonstrates the diversity of ethical responses that characterized the experiences of several black slaves who had experienced conversion. Sanders's work parallels Coleman's, because they both challenge contemporary black theologians concerning their tendency to universalize the slave experience by interpreting the narratives as having reflected unambiguous opposition to enslavement. Her distinctive contribution is twofold. First, like Coleman, she argues that contemporary black theology must seek to discover an interpretive framework for including a diversity of perspectives in the black theological discourse. Second, unlike the other contributors to this enterprise, Sanders is establishing the position of theological ethics as a dimension of the contemporary black theological task. Her contribution is a call to recognize the essentially multidisciplinary character of the future work of contemporary black theologians. And, finally, while Hopkins finds in the slave narratives an unambiguous commitment to the politics and culture of resistance, and Cummings discovers the Spirit of the black Christ of liberation, both Sanders and Coleman point to ambiguity in the narrative witness of the slaves. This tension is viewed by the collaborators as a necessary one, as well as a constructive part of the future work of black theology.

SLAVE NARRATIVES, BLACK THEOLOGY, AND WORSHIP

A common element in this work is the authors' recognition of the communal dimension of the black religious experience. Many of the narratives focus directly on the conversion or other religious experiences of black slaves; it is evident that the communal experience of God's Spirit was a basic ingredient to sustaining hope and enabling the freedom struggle throughout the slave community. Hopkins specifically notes that the "Invisible Institution" was the primordial black church that began in slavery. There are two basic insights that can be derived from their interpretation.

First, the narratives call attention to the essentially communal character of the Spirit. As black slaves gathered in "brush arbors" from sundown to sunup, and sang and danced to their "soul's satisfaction," they were able to create an enabling and empowering collective religious experience that became the basis of their hope. White preaching was not adequate, since it just told slaves to be good to their oppressors. In order to "feel de Spirret" it was necessary to gather in secret meeting places far from the eyes and ears of their human masters and serve God in their own way.

The common experience of chattel slavery was the historical context that provided black slaves with the contradictions that shaped their theological understanding of the world. In traditional theological terms it has been common to refer to the ecclesiastical community as the fellowship of believers or the communion of saints. In either case, the community members shared their common lives and resources in the presence of the Spirit. To dwell in the presence of the Spirit meant to share resources and life with other brothers and sisters in community where the life of God was experienced (Acts 2:42-47). These narratives affirm that the experiences of black slaves in community are no less than life in the Spirit. This is the reason for Cummings's insistence that the specific doctrine of the Spirit is necessary in order to link Jesus of Nazareth—the embodiment of God in the flesh—with the presence of the liberator Spirit in the slave experience. Because Jesus of Nazareth experienced crucifixion, and because they viewed their own suffering as tantamount to the crucifixion of Jesus, black slaves came to view Jesus as their companion and friend.

Rev. Bentley, the slave preacher, asserted that Christ came for the poor, "to us, and for our sakes."[10] Jesus as the embodiment of the God who has a heart for the oppressed was with black slaves as they struggled against slavery and white racism; he was their friend and companion and nobody knew about their troubles like Jesus, because he had experienced rejection, dehumanization, suffering, and crucifixion, just as they did each day on the plantations.

A contemporary black theology of liberation, therefore, will advance the claim that Jesus is the crucified people. In other words, the presence of the liberator Christ in the oppressed black community warrants our argument that we cannot speak of Jesus the Christ without speaking of Jesus, the presence of God, among those who daily experience suffering, and crucifixion, but who nevertheless celebrated the presence of the Spirit by disobeying their oppressors and struggling for freedom and justice. The life of the Spirit is authentically manifested in the community of the oppressed as they celebrate life, hope, and their expectation of total liberation.

Second, the narratives challenge contemporary black theologians to develop a specific understanding of worship in the life of an oppressed community. If, as seems self-evident in the varieties of testimonies, the secret meetings were the communal contexts of the slaves' encounters with the Spirit, then the narratives require that an understanding of the worship experiences of the community be devised in order to analyze them as a source for theological discourse. Prayers and sermons in the black religious experience become, then, another possible source for black theological discourse. In addition, the practices, sensibilities, and experiences of God in the black community can be seen as a crucial aspect of gaining access to the community's self-understanding of its life in the Spirit. This raises some important possibilities for evaluating the contemporary black church's understanding of its life in the Spirit in the light of the slave community's understanding of life in the Spirit as well as the biblical witness. The theological method of mutually critical correlations can provide us with some assistance here, as the process of determining the authenticity of each community's experience of God.

BLACK THEOLOGY AND THE GOD OF LIBERATION

This investigation of the slave narratives as a source for black theological discourse has contributed to contemporary black theology by acknowledging the diversity of the witnesses, while at the same time highlighting their common ground. The slaves' testimonies about God and liberation are two dimensions of their common experiences. The concept of God within the narratives persistently affirms God's sovereignty, righteousness, and justice. When emancipation came, for example, the nearly unanimous witness of the slave narratives is that God—a *just* and *righteous* and *sovereign* God—had heard their cries for freedom and had made it possible for them to be free.

Divine power, justice, and righteousness converged in the minds of black slaves to confirm their belief that chattel slavery was not consistent with the God of the Bible, Christianity, or of their own African high Gods. The chattel slavery they experienced in North America was ungodly and wrong, and eventually the Creator God acted to destroy those who perpetrated such evil and their institutions.

Black slaves' foundational understanding of God was that God was on the side of the poor and the oppressed—"the little ones"—and that God's righteousness and justice meant that the wicked would be the recipients of divine retribution.

In addition, earthly liberation from enslavement was viewed by slaves as being insolubly connected with individual salvation. Hopkins examines the story of the indomitable Uncle Silas, who persisted in inquiring of the Methodist preacher whether or not God was "gonna give us freedom 'long wid salvation?"[11] Uncle Silas, according to Hopkins, represents millions of blacks who rejected white people's interpretation of God in favor of their own view that freedom and God's salvation were closely linked.

In discussing the slave narrative views of eschatology Cummings has argued that one's personal encounter, in conversion, with the future of God—God's Spirit—is intimately interwoven with the slaves' capacity for heroism, courage, and hope in the midst of despair. To be assured that God has called your name—elected you as one of his chosen children—was to *know* that you were somebody; to *know* that you were not alone in the midst of evil; and, to *know* that God would vindicate that which is right in the world.

Sanders also affirms the link between personal salvation and the struggle for earthly liberation. Indeed, this is a common thread in all of the essays.

Closely related to the slaves' concept of God and liberation is their attitude toward evil in their situation. There is no need to rationalize the reality and presence of evil in the slaves' experience. Rather than debate the origin of evil, slaves recognized its reality in the power that their white masters and mistresses held over them. Some of them called white folks devils, precisely because they recognized the demonic power of white racism as it was manifested in the brutality of their oppressors. The genius of the African American slave experience is that it rejects a theological dialogue about the theodicy question; it acknowledges evil as a reality; and through imaginative mythopoetic and linguistic identification with Jesus the Crucified One combined with the traditional African world-view, it came to view the black slave community as the recipient of God's gracious Spirit, who would ensure ultimate liberation. Hence, the future of contemporary black theology need not be defined by a discussion of the theodicy question, but in the tradition of African slaves must seek to empower the eruption of God's liberating Spirit in the experiences of the contemporary black community.

CONCLUSION

In view of these three constellations of issues I will highlight areas of work within which contemporary black theologians should continue to advance collaboratively the black theological perspective. First, the slave narratives themselves need to be investigated in a more comprehensive manner by black scholars from the diversity of disciplines. Comparative religionists, philosophers, anthropologists, sociologists, historians, theologians, and ethicists, among many others, will make valuable contributions to the slave narratives by a concerted attempt to interpret the mythopoetic and linguistic world that emerges from their experiences. Black theology will be enhanced immensely by the valuable contributions that can come from dialogue with these other disciplines.

Second, the areas of hermeneutics, linguistics, and theological methodology must be further developed. It is clear that the writers of this work are engaged in questions of methodology and hermeneutics.

Third, a comprehensive and comparative study of the varieties of sources of black religio-cultural traditions ought to be pursued, in order to evaluate the notions of God, Jesus, the Spirit, and human purpose in the various sources. How, for example, do the testimonies of the slave narratives compare with other literary expressions or with black preachers' sermons in the African American experience?

Fourth, a detailed study of worship in the black experience will be a valuable contribution to the work of black theology as we struggle to discover the means through which to convey the primordial experiences of the slaves' encounter with the Spirit to the present age.

And, finally, this theological and ethical interpretation of the slave narratives is a confirmation for the contemporary black Christian community that the biographies of black people — black testimonies — are as significant as sources of the *biography* of God, on theological grounds. Christian theology, the eminent theologian C. S. Song has argued,

> is a biography of God from the perspective of the Christian faith. It is an effort to give an account of God against the background of the Christian traditions. It is an attempt to let God speak for God's self on the basis of what Christians perceive to be signs of God's activity in human community. ... If theology is a biography of God, there must be as many theologies as biographies of God. *This is one of the most exciting discoveries of our day.*[12]

Contemporary black theology from its inception has identified itself as a black Christian theology of liberation. While the debate concerning the specific character of the black religious experience, or the function of theological categories, may continue, black theologians must continue to insist that black theology is Christian. While black theologians may acknowledge the diverse religio-cultural sources and the ambivalence and ambiguity of the black witnesses, it is nevertheless the task of the black Christian theologians of liberation to explicate the meaning of the gospel of Jesus Christ from the perspective of the experiences of black oppressed people. This is a specific vocation that requires the theologians to acknowledge both their Christian presuppositions and their grounding in the black freedom struggle. This means, for us as it means for Song, that we have discovered the biography and theology of God in the testimonies of African American slaves, who believed that God was present in their experience. The Jesus of history is not simply an ancient personage limited to first-century Palestine, but the presence of God among the crucified ones of this world. Jesus was crucified in the black slave experience and becomes an important starting point for contemporary black Christian theology that aims to challenge the hegemonic God of white privilege and to establish the basis for a counter-hegemonic black God whose nature is justice and righteousness, and whose heart is for the crucified ones.

NOTES

INTRODUCTION

1. The "Invisible Institution" is the name scholars have given to the secret worship services of black American slaves prior to the Civil War.

2. George P. Rawick, ed., *The American Slave: A Composite Autobiography*, 41 vols. (Westport, Conn.: Greenwood Publishing Company, 1972, 1977, 1979).

3. Charles L. Perdue, Jr., et al., eds., *Weevils in the Wheat: Interviews with Virginia Ex-Slaves* (Bloomington, Ind., and London: Indiana University Press, 1980; originally published by the University Press of Virginia in 1976); Georgia Writers' Project, *Drums and Shadows: Survival Studies Among the Georgia Coastal Negroes* (Westport, Conn.: Greenwood Publishing Company, 1973, 1976; originally published by the University of Georgia Press in 1940); Lyle Saxon, et al., compilers, *Gumbo Ya-Ya: Folk Tales of Louisiana* (Gretna, La.: Pelican, 1987). The American Freedmen's Inquiry Commission 1863 results are found in the National Archives.

4. Ulrich B. Phillips, *Life and Labor in the Old South* (Boston: Little, Brown, 1929), p. 219.

5. Eugene D. Genovese, *Roll, Jordan, Roll: The World the Slaves Made* (New York: Pantheon Books/Random House, 1972); Rawick, *From Sundown to Sunup: The Making of the Black Community* (Westport, Conn.: Greenwood Publishing Company, 1973); John W. Blassingame, *The Slave Community: Plantation Life in the Antebellum South* (New York: Oxford University Press, 1972).

6. Other collections of primary material by the slaves are B. A. Botkin, ed., *Lay My Burden Down: A Folk History of Slavery* (Chicago: University of Chicago Press, 1945); Norman R. Yetman, ed., *Voices from Slavery: The Life of American Slaves — in the Words of 100 Men and Women Who Lived It and Many Years Later Talked About It* (New York: Holt, Rinehart and Winston, 1970); Gilbert Osofsky, ed., *Puttin' On*

Ole Massa: The Slave Narratives of Henry Bibb, William Wells Brown, and Solomon Northup (New York: Harper & Row, 1969); Henry Louis Gates, Jr., ed., *Six Women's Slave Narratives* (New York: Oxford University Press, 1988); John W. Blassingame, ed., *Slave Testimony: Two Centuries of Letters, Speeches, Interviews, and Autobiographies* (Baton Rouge, La.: Louisiana State University Press, 1977); and John B. Cade, "Out of the Mouth of Ex-Slaves," *Journal of Negro History* 20 (1935): 294-337.

Important secondary sources are Marion Wilson Starling's definitive work, *The Slave Narrative: Its Place in American History* (Washington, D.C.: Howard University, 1988); George P. Rawick, *From Sundown to Sunup: The Making of the Black Community* (Westport, Conn.: Greenwood Publishing Company, 1972); Paul D. Escott, *Slavery Remembered: A Record of Twentieth-Century Slave Narratives* (Chapel Hill, N.C.: The University of North Carolina Press, 1979); Charles T. Davis and Henry Louis Gates, Jr., eds., *The Slave's Narrative* (New York: Oxford University Press, 1985); and William L. Andrews, *To Tell a Free Story: The First Century of Afro-American Autobiography, 1760-1865* (Urbana, Ill.: University of Illinois Press, 1988).

7. See secondary sources listed above, note 6.

8. Starling, p. 1.

9. In his pioneering work *Slave Religion: The "Invisible Institution" in the Antebellum South* (New York: Oxford University Press, 1978), Albert J. Raboteau uses the slave narratives as a major source for his text. However, Raboteau's explicit purpose is, strictly speaking, not theological but religious. He seeks to answer the following questions: "What were the origins of black religion in America? What aspects of African religions were retained by the slaves? How did evangelization and conversion of African slaves to Christianity take place? What was the nature of the religion to which the slave was converted?" (p. xi).

10. For extended reviews of the history of contemporary black theology, see James H. Cone, *For My People: Black Theology and the Black Church* (Maryknoll, N.Y.: Orbis Books, 1984), chap. 1; Gayraud S. Wilmore and James H. Cone, eds., *Black Theology: A Documentary History, 1966-1979* (Maryknoll, N.Y.: Orbis Books, 1979), pp. 4ff.; Gayraud Wilmore, "Black Theology: Review and Assessment," *Voices from the Third World*, vol. 5, no. 2 (December 1982), pp. 3-16; and Dwight N. Hopkins, *Black Theology USA and South Africa: Politics, Culture, and Liberation* (Maryknoll, N.Y.: Orbis Books, 1989), chap. 1.

11. This young movement saw its first theological text published with James H. Cone's *Black Theology and Black Power* (New York: Seabury Press, 1969).

12. See various articles by Kelly Brown, Katie Cannon, Jualynne Dodson, Cheryl Townsend Gilkes, Jacquelyn Grant, Cheryl Sanders, Renita Weems, and Delores Williams.

13. Since around 1976 the Ecumenical Association of Third World Theologians has been the most organized and active world forum for the development of liberation theologies. The proceedings of its various continental and world assemblies have been published by Orbis Books.

14. Will Coleman (doctoral candidate at the Graduate Theological Union, Berkeley), Dwight N. Hopkins (Assistant Professor of Religious and Ethnic Studies at Santa Clara University), and George C. L. Cummings (Associate Professor of Systematic Theology at the American Baptist Seminary of the West, Berkeley) formed the Forum. James Noel (Professor at San Francisco Theological Seminary) joined later.

15. From an anonymous slave narrative quoted in *God Struck Me Dead: Religious Conversion Experiences and Autobiographies of Ex-Slaves*, ed. Clifton H. Johnson (Philadelphia, Penn., and Boston, Mass.: Pilgrim Press, 1969; originally published by Fisk University in 1945), pp. 16-17.

1. SLAVE THEOLOGY IN THE "INVISIBLE INSTITUTION"

1. Thomas Wentworth Higginson, *Army Life in a Black Regiment* (New York: W. W. Norton, 1984; originally published 1869), p. 49. Higginson commanded "the first slave regiment mustered into the service of the United States during the . . . civil war" (p. 27).

2. Charles L. Perdue, Jr., et al., eds., *Weevils in the Wheat: Interviews with Virginia Ex-Slaves* (Bloomington, Ind., and London: Indiana University Press, 1980; originally published by the University Press of Virginia in 1976), p. 62.

3. For a review of the European trading in Africans and the implantation of Africans in the New World, see Vincent Harding, *There Is a River: The Black Struggle for Freedom in America* (New York: Harcourt Brace Jovanovich, 1981), chaps. 1-2; and John Hope Franklin, *From Slavery to Freedom: A History of Negro Americans* (New York: Alfred A. Knopf, 1980), chaps. 3-5.

4. Ogbu U. Kalu, "Church Presence in Africa: A Historical Analysis of the Evangelization Process," in *African Theology En Route*, ed. Kofi Appiah-Kubi and Sergio Torres (Maryknoll, N.Y.: Orbis Books, 1979), p. 18. This quotation comes from a white missionary at the beginning of the twentieth century. However, these theological views were held since the first European contact with Africa.

5. John S. Mbiti, *Concepts of God in Africa* (London: SPCK, 1970), p. 6. Also see Gwinyai H. Muzorewa, *The Origins and Development of*

African Theology (Maryknoll, N.Y.: Orbis Books, 1985), p. 9.

6. Mbiti, pp. 8-21.

7. Mbiti, pp. 31-76. Also see Muzorewa, p. 10.

8. Mercy Amba Oduyoye, "The Value of African Religious Beliefs and Practices for Christian Theology," in Appiah-Kubi and Torres, p. 111. Also see Muzorewa, p. 17; E. Thomas Lawson, *Religions of Africa* (New York: Harper & Row, 1985), p. 97; and Mbiti, *African Religions and Philosophy* (Garden City, N.Y.: Anchor Books, 1970), p. 141.

9. Oduyoye, p. 111.

10. For treatments of the African influence in slave religion, see Gayraud Wilmore, *Black Religion and Black Radicalism: An Interpretation of the Religious History of Afro-American People* (Maryknoll, N.Y.: Orbis Books, 1983), chap. 1; and Albert J. Raboteau, *Slave Religion: The "Invisible Institution" in the Antebellum South* (New York: Oxford University Press, 1980), chaps. 1 and 2.

11. Becky Ilsey, quoted in Lawrence Levine, *Black Culture and Black Consciousness: Afro-American Folk Thought from Slavery to Freedom* (New York: Oxford University Press, 1981), p. 41.

12. Archie Booker, quoted in Perdue, pp. 52-53.

13. Charles Grandy, quoted in Perdue, p. 119.

14. Arthur Greene, quoted in Perdue, pp. 124-25.

15. Levi Pollard, quoted in Perdue, p. 230.

16. Ex-slave quotations come from James Mellon, ed., *Bullwhip Days: The Slaves Remember, An Oral History* (New York: Weidenfeld & Nicolson, 1988), p. 190; and Norman R. Yetman, *Life Under the "Peculiar Institution": Selections from the Slave Narrative Collection* (New York: Holt, Rinehart and Winston, 1970), pp. 53, 231, 56.

17. Quotations are found in Mellon, pp. 186-87, 194-95. Other ex-slave references to the cultural dimension of the "Invisible Institution" can be found in Levine, pp. 41, 42; Perdue, p. 100 (" 'Cause we wanted to serve God in our own way. You see, 'legion needs a little motion—specially if you gwine feel de spirret"), p. 322; Clifton H. Johnson, ed., *God Struck Me Dead: Religious Conversion Experiences and Autobiographies of Ex-Slaves* (Philadelphia: Pilgrim Press, 1969), p. 153; and Eugene D. Genovese, *Roll, Jordan, Roll: The World the Slaves Made* (New York: Pantheon Books/Random House, 1972), p. 214 ("White folks can't pray right to de black man's God. Can't nobody do it for you. You got to call on God yourself when de spirit tell you.").

18. Perdue, pp. 93, 161. Throughout the slave narratives one discovers this reference to the turned-over pot. Also see Yetman, p. 229.

19. West Turner, quoted in Perdue, p. 290.

20. Ishrael Massie, quoted in Perdue, p. 208.

21. Perdue, pp. 183, 230, 150, 71.

22. Yetman, p. 33; Mellon, pp. 196-97.

23. See John W. Blassingame, ed., *Slave Testimony: Two Centuries of Letters, Speeches, Interviews, and Autobiographies* (Baton Rouge, La.: Louisiana State University Press, 1977), p. 411.

24. B. A. Botkin, ed., *Lay My Burden Down: A Folk History of Slavery* (Chicago: University of Chicago Press, 1957), p. 91. References for quotations on white sermons and catechisms can be found in Perdue, pp. 241, 183; Harriet A. Jacobs, *Incidents in the Life of a Slave Girl, Written by Herself* (Cambridge, Mass.: Harvard University Press, 1987), pp. 68-69; and Frederick Douglass, *Life and Times of Frederick Douglass* (New York: Collier Books, 1973; the first condensed version originally published in 1845), p. 157.

25. Yetman, pp. 231-32. Also review Levine, pp. 41-42, 46; and Perdue, pp. 207, 290.

26. Other ex-slave narratives substantiate white theological hubris. See Botkin, pp. 25, 94; Yetman, pp. 180-81, 262.

27. Charles Davenport, quoted in Yetman, p. 75.

28. Henry Bibb, *Narrative of the Life and Adventures of Henry Bibb, An American Slave, Written by Himself* (Philadelphia, Penn.: Historic Publications, n.d.), p. 114. Bibb originally published his book in 1849.

29. For a sampling of slave accounts of praying for freedom, see Perdue, pp. 94, 115; Mellon, pp. 190, 196; Yetman pp. 177, 308, 312; and Blassingame, pp. 661, 700.

30. Solomon Northup, *Twelve Years a Slave* (New York: Dover Publications, 1970; originally published in 1854), p. 68.

31. Botkin, p. 26.

32. Charles Grandy, quoted in Perdue, p. 115.

33. J. W. Lindsey, quoted in Blassingame, p. 404. Also note Horace Muse's comment, "No res' fer niggers 'till God he step in an' put a stop to de white folks meanness," in Perdue, p. 216.

34. The theological view of "momentary God" comes from a narrative in Botkin, p. 34. The reference to Ole Ant Sissy comes from Perdue, p. 127.

35. Miles Mark Fisher, *Negro Slave Songs in the United States* (Secaucus, N.J.: The Citadel Press, 1978), p. 54.

36. James L. Bradley, quoted in Blassingame, p. 690.

37. Blassingame, pp. 125-26.

38. Perdue, pp. 72, 33; Yetman, p. 48; and Botkin, p. 178.

39. Ishrael Massie, quoted in Perdue, p. 206. Also see another ex-bondsman's similar claim on pp. 80, 93-94.

40. Perdue, pp. 274, 1. Other references to the theology of the

heaven-hell kingdoms can be found in Mellon, p. 178, and Botkin, p. 121. George White stated: "Dey ask me de other day if I thought any of de slaveholders was in heaven an' I told 'em no 'cause dey was too mean" (Perdue, p. 311).

41. Botkin, p. 163; Perdue, pp. 93-94.

42. Yetman pp. 113-14. For a description of the slaves' image of Jubilee, see Fisher, p. 121. For the slaves' self-interpretation as the children of God, see Yetman, p. 205.

43. Perdue, p. 184.

44. Levine, p. 28.

45. Fisher, pp. 66ff; and John Lovell, Jr., *Black Song: The Forge and the Flame* (New York: Paragon House Publishers, 1986), pp. 125, 191, 228, 379. For further examination of the theological and religious thought of Rev. Nat Turner, see Stephen B. Oates, *The Fires of Jubilee: Nat Turner's Fierce Rebellion* (New York: The New American Library, 1975). For Harriet Tubman's theology, review Sarah Bradford, *Harriet Tubman: The Moses of Her People* (Secaucus, N.J.: The Citadel Press, 1961).

46. The slaves considered all aspects of Jesus as prophetic in the sense of subverting white Christianity. Therefore I do not develop a specific section on Jesus' prophetic office.

47. Levine, p. 43; William F. Allen, Charles P. Ware, and Lucy M. Garrison, eds., *Slave Songs of the United States* (New York: Books for Libraries Press, 1971, originally published 1867), p. 11.

48. Fisher, pp. 16-17.

49. See Harding; Wilmore.

50. Jacobs, p. 70; Fisher, p. 48.

51. Yetman, p. 228.

52. Allen, Ware, and Garrison, pp. 70, 97.

53. Yetman, p. 225.

54. Former slave Phillip Ward recalls, "Marsa bringing his son . . . down to the cabin. They both took her [a black woman]—the father showing the son what it was all about" (Perdue, p. 301).

55. Rev. Bentley, quoted in Levine, p. 49.

56. Charles Moses, quoted in Mellon, p. 182.

57. James L. Bradley, quoted in Blassingame, p. 689.

58. Bibb, p. 17.

59. Thomas Likers, quoted in Blassingame, p. 395.

60. Arthur Greene, quoted in Perdue, pp. 125, 153.

61. Fisher, p. 74.

62. Botkin, p. 176. For the reference to the black woman plowing in the field, see Botkin, p. 175.

63. Perdue, pp. 55-56.

64. Robert Ellett, quoted in Perdue, p. 85. For fuller details on the theological significance of the Underground Railroad, see Bradford.

65. Yetman, p. 53. Other quotations can be found in Botkin, p. 26, and Perdue, pp. 245, 226.

66. Perdue, p. 124.

67. Genovese, p. 605.

68. Ibid. p. 602.

69. Sarah Fitzpatrick, quoted in Blassingame, p. 652.

70. Lunsford Lane, quoted in Gilbert Osofsky, ed., *Puttin' On Ole Massa: The Slave Narratives of Henry Bibb, William Wells Brown, and Solomon Northup* (New York: Harper & Row, 1969), p. 9. The quotation from Henry Bibb comes from Bibb, p. 17.

71. Robert Smalls, quoted in Blassingame, p. 377.

72. Ishrael Massie, quoted in Perdue, p. 210.

73. Mrs. Jennie Patterson, quoted in Perdue, p. 220.

74. Perdue, p. 128.

2. THE SLAVE NARRATIVES AS A SOURCE OF BLACK THEOLOGICAL DISCOURSE

1. See, for example, James H. Cone, *God of the Oppressed* (New York: Seabury Press, 1975). Cone argues that the theologian "must imagine his way into the environment and the ethos of the black slaves, probing the language and rhythm of a people who had to feel their way along the course of slavery" (p. 11). Cone challenges theologians to look at the slave narratives that introduce us to the world of the black slaves as a source for black theology (p. 27).

See also Gayraud Wilmore, *Black Religion and Black Radicalism* (Garden City, N.Y.: Anchor Books/Doubleday, 1973). He calls on black theologians to return to black sources (pp. 298-302).

See also Charles Long, *Interpretation of Religion* (Philadelphia, Penn.: Fortress Press, 1986). Long calls for the evolution of a theology of the opaque derived by contemplating "a narrative of meaning that is commensurate with the quality of beauty that was fired in the crucible of slavery" (p. 1).

2. George P. Rawick, ed., *The American Slave: A Composite Autobiography*, Supplement, Series 1 (Westport, Conn.: Greenwood Publishing Company, 1977), vol. 5, p. 127.

3. Rawick, vol. 4, p. 170.

4. See *God Struck Me Dead: Religious Conversion Experiences and Autobiographies of Ex-Slaves*, ed. Clifton H. Johnson (Philadelphia,

Penn., and Boston, Mass.: Pilgrim Press, 1969; originally published by Fisk University in 1945), pp. 15, 19, 21, 59-60.

5. Nancy Williams, quoted in Charles L. Perdue, Jr., et al., eds., *Weevils in the Wheat: Interviews with Virginia Ex-Slaves* (Bloomington, Ind.: Indiana University Press, 1976), p. 320.

6. Mechal Sobel, *Travelin' On: The Slave Journey to an Afro-Baptist Faith* (Princeton, N.J.: Princeton University Press, 1988), p. xxiii.

7. Cornelius Garner, quoted in Perdue, p. 100.

8. James Mellon, ed., *Bullwhip Days: The Slaves Remember* (New York: Weidenfeld & Nicolson, 1988), pp. 194-95.

9. William Moore, quoted in George P. Rawick, ed., *The American Slave: A Composite Autobiography*, Supplement, Series 2 (Westport, Conn.: Greenwood Publishing Company, 1979), vol. 7, p. 2766.

10. Mellon, p. 190.

11. Barney Alford, quoted in Rawick, Supplement 1, vol. 6, p. 41.

12. Ellen Butler, quoted in Rawick, Supplement 1, vol. 4, p. 411.

13. Jacob Branch, quoted in Rawick, Supplement 2, vol. 2, p. 411.

14. Howard Thurman, *The Negro Spiritual Speaks of Life and Death* (New York: Harper & Row, 1947), p. 12. Approximately twenty-five years later James H. Cone picked up this theme in his important text, *The Spirituals and the Blues* (New York: Seabury Press, 1972).

15. Carey Davenport, quoted in Rawick, Supplement 2, vol. 4, p. 1052.

16. Anderson Edwards, quoted in Rawick, Supplement 2, vol. 4, p. 1262.

17. John White, quoted in Rawick, Supplement 2, vol. 7, pp. 325-26.

18. Joe Oliver, quoted in Rawick, Supplement 2, vol. 8, p. 2979.

19. Jane Pyatt, quoted in Perdue, p. 235.

20. Charlie Bowen, quoted in Rawick, Supplement 2, vol. 2, p. 349.

21. George Cato, quoted in Mellon, p. 460.

22. Carl E. Braaten, "The Kingdom of God and Life Everlasting," in *Christian Theology: Introduction to Its Traditions and Tasks*, ed. Peter Hodgson and Robert H. King (Philadelphia, Penn.: Fortress Press, 1982), p. 329.

23. Anderson Edwards, quoted in Rawick, Supplement 2, vol. 4, p. 1266.

24. Ibid. p. 1262.

25. John Crawford, quoted in Rawick, vol. 4, Part I, p. 966.

26. George King, quoted in Rawick, vol. 7, Part I, p. 165.

27. Rawick, vol. 18, p. 118.

28. Jack Maddox, quoted in Mellon, p. 115.

29. Frederick Douglass, *The Life and Times of Frederick Douglass*, rev. ed. 1892 (London: Collier-Macmillan, 1962), p. 41.

30. Sarah Bradford, *Harriet Tubman: The Moses of Her People* (New York: Corinth Books, 1961), p. 30.

31. Johnson, pp. 165-66.

32. Johnson, pp. 59-60.

33. Johnson, p. 122.

34. For the concept of counter-hegemonic culture, see Cornel West, *Prophesy Deliverance: An Afro-American Revolutionary Christianity* (Philadelphia, Penn.: Westminster Press, 1982), p. 120. West expands Antonio Gramsci's concept of hegemonic culture and defines counter-hegemonic culture as that which "represents genuine opposition to hegemonic culture; ... fosters an alternative set of habits, sensibilities, and world views that cannot possibly be realized within the perimeters of the established order." I link religion and culture in light of their equally significant role in either legitimating the status quo or supporting the evolution of oppositional values and institutions that stand against the established order.

35. Rawick, Supplement 2, vol. 8, part 7, p. 2979.

36. John White, quoted in Rawick, Supplement 2, vol. 7, pp. 325-26.

37. John Crawford, quoted in Rawick, Supplement 2, vol. 4, p. 966.

38. Cone, *God of the Oppressed*, pp. 108-37.

39. Mollie Dawson, quoted in Mellon, p. 428.

3. "COMING THROUGH 'LIGION"

1. The excerpt is taken from a series of interviews I held with my paternal grandmother, Alice Coleman, regarding the religious heritage of our family.

2. See Albert J. Raboteau, *Slave Religion: The "Invisible Institution" in the Antebellum South* (New York: Oxford University Press, 1978). This book is a classic work on the development of slave religion in the antebellum South, both within and apart from the institutional churches—European and/or African American. In general, the expression "Invisible Institution" refers to the secret religious meetings of African American slaves.

3. These insights have been gleaned from the major works of Paul Ricoeur on hermeneutical theory and will be discussed later in this paper. Those writings include *Hermeneutics and the Human Sciences* and *Interpretation Theory: Discourse and the Surplus of Meaning* (Fort Worth, Tex.: The Texas Christian University Press, 1976); *The Rule of*

Metaphor: Multi-disciplinary Studies of Creation of Meaning in Language, trans. Robert Czerny with Kathleen McLaughlin and John Costello, S.J. (Toronto and Buffalo: University of Toronto Press, 1977; his translation of *La Metaphore Vive* (Paris: Editions du Seuil, 1975); *Time and Narrative*, vol. 1, trans. Kathleen McLaughlin and David Pellauer (Chicago: University of Chicago Press, 1984; his translation of *Temps et Récit*, vol. 1 (Paris: Editions du Seuil, 1983); *Time and Narrative*, vol. 2, trans. Kathleen McLaughlin and David Pellauer (Chicago: University of Chicago Press, 1985; his translation of *Temps et Récit*, vol. 2 (Paris: Editions du Seuil, 1984); *Time and Narrative*, vol. 3, trans. Kathleen Blamey and David Pellauer (Chicago: University of Chicago Press, 1988; his translation of *Temps et Récit*, vol. 3 (Paris: Editions du Seuil, 1985).

4. Here the concern is with the autonomy of the text in presenting the world-view of African American slaves. On this issue see Paul Ricoeur, *Hermeneutics and the Human Sciences: Essays on Language, Action and Interpretation*, ed. and trans. John B. Thompson (Paris, London, New York: Maison des Sciences de l'Homme and Cambridge University Press, 1981), pp. 91, 108, 165.

5. Black theologians such as James H. Cone, Gayraud S. Wilmore, and J. Deotis Roberts have argued for the use of resources from the total experience of African American people in black theology. These include literary materials such as slave narratives, folklore, and spirituals that describe their responses to slavery. James H. Cone, *The Spirituals and the Blues* (New York: Seabury Press, 1972), pp. 3, 6; Gayraud S. Wilmore, *Black Religion and Black Radicalism: An Interpretation of the Religious History of Afro-American People*, 2d rev. ed. (Maryknoll, N.Y.: Orbis Books, 1983; originally published in the C. Eric Lincoln Series on Black Religion by Anchor Press/Doubleday, 1973), pp. 234-41; James Deotis Roberts, *Black Theology Today: Liberation and Contextualization*, Toronto Studies in Theology, vol. 12 (New York and Toronto: The Edwin Mellen Press, 1983), p. 196.

6. For this essay I have selected narratives from the Carolinas and Georgia region. My rationale for this decision is a desire to stay as close as possible to the initial slave ports, because my theory is that the "African substratum" (Wilmore, p. 15ff) in the United States is most prevalent in those coastal regions known as the Gullah and Geechee territories. The testimonies used in this paper are from supplemental volumes 3 and 11 of *The American Slave: A Composite Autobiography*, 41 vols., George P. Rawick, ed. (Westport, Conn.: Greenwood Publishing Company, 1977). There is also an excellent index to this series: *Index to The American Slave*, ed. Donald M. Jacobs, Contributions in

Afro-American and African Studies, no. 65 (Westport, Conn.: Greenwood Publishing Company, 1981).

In addition to the general introduction to *The American Slave*, questions concerning methodology, criteria, and authenticity with respect to the process of compilation and norms governing the final composition of African American slave narratives should be referred to the following related works: George P. Rawick, *From Sundown to Sunup: The Making of the Black Community* (Westport, Conn.: Greenwood Publishing Company, 1972), pp. xiii-xxi, 163-78; B. A. Botkin, ed., *Lay My Burden Down: A Folk History of Slavery* (Athens, Ga., and London: University of Georgia Press, 1989; originally published in 1945 by the University of Chicago Press), pp. vii-xiv, 271-86; Charles Perdue, et al., *Weevils in the Wheat: Interviews with Virginia Ex-Slaves*, (Bloomington, Ind., and London: Indiana University Press, 1980; originally published by the University Press of Virginia in 1976), pp. xi-xlv, 351-94; and Norman R. Yetman, *Life Under the "Peculiar Institution": Selections from the Slave Narrative Collection* (New York: Holt, Rinehart and Winston, 1970), pp. 1-6, 339-58.

7. Rawick, Supplement 1, vol. 11, p. 179.

8. John S. Mbiti, *An Introduction to African Religion* (London: Heinemann Educational Books Ltd., 1975), chap. 7, "The Spirits."

9. Rawick, Supplement 1, vol. 11, pp. 30-31.

10. Raboteau, p. 12.

11. Rawick, Supplement 1, vol. 11, p. 223.

12. See Wilmore, pp. 4-28; Lawrence W. Levine, *Black Culture and Black Consciousness: Afro-American Folk Thought from Slavery to Freedom* (Oxford, London, New York: Oxford University Press, 1977), pp. 55-80, 60.

13. Rawick, Supplement 1, vol. 3, pp. 135, 136-37.

14. Ibid. p. 137.

15. The belief that a person has more than one spirit has Afrocentric roots. Many Africans, such as the Yoruba of West Africa, believe in multiple souls that function differently within one's personality. Likewise, Haitian Voodooists believe everyone has two souls: 1) the *gros bon ange*, who travels during our sleep; and 2) the *petit bon ange*, who leaves us when we die. See William Bascom, *Ifa Divination: Communication Between Gods and Men in West Africa* (Bloomington and London: Indiana University Press, 1969), p. 114; Claude Planson, *Voodoo: Rituals and Possessions*, ed. Pierre Horay (Paris: Passage Dauphine, 1975), p. 40.

16. Rawick, Supplement 1, vol. 3, pp. 138-39, pp. 140-41, 141.

17. There are hundreds of folklore beliefs and formulas related to

either curing or harming someone else in *Hoodoo, Conjuration, Witchcraft, Rootwork: Beliefs Accepted by Many Negroes and White Persons, These Being Orally Recorded Among Blacks and Whites*, 5 vols., comp. Harry Middleton Hyatt. Volumes 1 and 2 were published in Hannibal, Missouri, by Western Publishing, Inc., 1970. Volumes 3, 4, and 5 were published in Cambridge, Maryland, by Western Publishing Company, 1973, 1974, and 1978, respectively. For more examples of folklore and Africanisms among African American slaves in the Georgia coastal region, see *Drums and Shadows: Survival Studies Among the Georgia Coastal Negroes*, Georgia Writers' Project (Westport, Conn.: Greenwood Publishing Company, 1973, 1976; originally published by the University of Georgia Press, Athens, Ga., in 1940).

18. For Africanisms on the importance of going to a good conjurer in order to undo the work performed by an evil one, see *Drums and Shadows: Survival Studies Among the Georgia Coastal Negroes*, pp. 232-33.

19. Numerous examples of this phenomenon are recorded in *God Struck Me Dead: Religious Conversion Experiences and Autobiographies of Ex-Slaves*, ed. Clifton H. Johnson (Philadelphia, Penn., and Boston, Mass.: Pilgrim Press, 1969; originally published by Fisk University in 1945).

20. Rawick, Supplement 1, vol. 11, p. 281.

21. Rawick, Supplement 1, vol. 3, p. 257.

22. Ibid. p. 258.

23. Ibid. p. 259.

24. Rawick, Supplement 1, vol. 11, p. 117.

25. For Carl G. Jung, the alchemical process of discovering the "philosopher's stone" is analogous to that of individuation, or coming to realize a balanced wholeness within oneself. Also, this is a means for reconciling opposite traits within one's own personality. Often dream symbolism provides clues to how this might be accomplished. See Carl G. Jung, *Mysterium Coniunctionis: An Inquiry into the Separation and Synthesis of Psychic Opposites in Alchemy*, trans. R.F.C. Hull, 2d ed., Bollingen Series 20 (Princeton, N.J.: Princeton University Press, 1963, 1970, 1977), pp. xiii-xix; idem, *Psychology and Alchemy*, trans. R.F.C. Hull, Bollingen Series 20 (Princeton, N.J.: Princeton University Press, 1953, 1980). See also Mircea Eliade, *The Forge and the Crucible: The Origins of Alchemy*, trans. Stephen Corrin (New York and Evanston, Ill.: Harper & Row, 1962), pp. 148-52.

26. Shamanism is experienced cross-culturally. In it, one undergoes an initiatory process, through various individual and communal techniques, in order to emerge as a religious leader and healer in a given

community. Usually it is instigated by a dream or vision like the one in this narrative. "Doc" Richmond, since he is living under a Christian framework, becomes a minister. See Mircea Eliade, *Shamanism: Archaic Techniques of Ecstacy*, trans. Willard R. Trask (Princeton, N.J.: Princeton University Press, 1964), especially pp. 1-33.

27. Rawick, Supplement 1, vol. 3, p. 1, 2, 3, 4-5, 5-6, 14.

28. Rawick, Supplement 1, vol. 11, pp. 180-81.

29. Wilmore, pp. 6, 12.

30. Ibid. p. 11.

31. Zora Neale Hurston, *The Sanctified Church: The Folklore Writings of Zora Neale Hurston* (Berkeley: Turtle Island Foundation, 1981), p. 91; Raboteau, pp. 59-75.

32. Ricoeur, *Interpretation Theory: Discourse and the Surplus of Meaning*, pp. 45-46, 55-57; *Hermeneutics and the Human Sciences*, pp. 169, 181.

33. Ricoeur, *Hermeneutics and the Human Sciences*, p. 43.

34. *The Philosophy of Paul Ricoeur: An Anthology of His Works*, ed. Charles E. Reagan and David Stewart (Boston: Beacon Press, 1978), p. 223.

35. Ricoeur, "Biblical Hermeneutics," *Semeia* 4 (1975), pp. 122-28; also cited in Sallie McFague, *Metaphorical Theology: Models of God in Religious Language* (Philadelphia, Penn.: Fortress Press, 1982), pp. 46-47. Ricoeur's analysis of the parabolic "pattern" is applicable to other literary genres that display a similar configuration. I maintain that many African American slave narratives possess this trait.

36. Ricoeur, *Interpretation Theory*, p. 20.

37. On the relationship between interior experiences and oral discourse, see Reagan and Stewart, p. 230.

38. Ibid. p. 237.

39. Ibid. p. 231.

40. Ibid. p. 232.

41. Ibid. p. 233; also see Ricoeur, *Interpretation Theory*, pp. 55-57.

42. Ricoeur, *The Symbolism of Evil*, trans. Emerson Buchanan (Boston: Beacon Press, 1969), p. 350.

43. Ricoeur, *Time and Narrative*, vol. 1, p. 65; *Time and Narrative*, vol. 2, p. 37.

44. For Ricoeur, both historical and fictional narratives have a structural unity because each develops a plot, a narrative intentionality, one through the selective arrangement of historical data, the other from the imagination of its author. See Ricoeur, *Hermeneutics and the Human Sciences*, p. 294; *Time and Narrative*, vol. 2, pp. 156-57.

45. Ricoeur, *Time and Narrative*, vol. 1, pp. 66-67.

46. Paul Ricoeur, *Essays on Biblical Interpretation*, ed. Lewis S. Mudge (Philadelphia: Penn.: Fortress Press, 1980), p. 108; Ricoeur, *Hermeneutics and the Human Sciences*, p. 192. In much of Ricoeur's writing on appropriation it seems that only the individual can take this final step in the hermeneutical process. But there appears to be a suggestion in the direction of a communal "application" of narratives; for example, in the case where the community identifies with and applies a narrative to itself such that the narrative becomes, for it, its actual history (*Time and Narrative*, vol. 3, pp. 246-47). Given the communal self-understanding of most African Americans, a communal appropriation is indispensable for the hermeneutical process.

47. The nuance between "explanation" and "understanding" is that of both distinguishing and appreciating the relationship between the structure of the text and its meaning. See Ricoeur, *Hermeneutics and Human Sciences*, pp. 145ff.

4. LIBERATION ETHICS IN THE EX-SLAVE INTERVIEWS

1. Ralph B. Potter, *War and Moral Discourse* (Richmond: John Knox Press, 1969), pp. 23-24.

2. George P. Rawick, ed., *The American Slave: A Composite Autobiography*, 41 vols. (Westport, Conn.: Greenwood Publishing Company, 1972, 1977, 1979).

3. Pet Franks, quoted in Rawick, p. 793.

4. Franks, p. 797.

5. Franks, p. 795.

6. Sister Kelly, quoted in Rawick, vol. 18, p. 161.

7. Kelly, p. 161.

8. Kelly, p. 161.

9. Kelly, p. 162.

10. Kelly, p. 162.

11. Wesley Little, quoted in Rawick, Supplement 1, vol. 8, p. 1317.

12. Little, pp. 1318-19.

13. Little, pp. 1321-22.

14. Little, p. 1320.

15. Little, p. 1317.

16. Little, p. 1322.

17. Laura Redmoun, quoted in Rawick, Supplement 2, vol. 8, p. 3265.

18. Redmoun, p. 3268.

19. Redmoun, p. 3270.

20. Redmoun, p. 3266.

21. Potter, p. 23.

22. *The American Heritage Dictionary of the English Language* (New York: American Heritage Publishing Co., 1975).

23. Franks, p. 795.

24. Franks, p. 798.

25. Franks, pp. 793-94.

26. Franks, p. 800.

27. Dora Franks, quoted in Rawick, Supplement 1, vol. 7, pp. 789-90.

28. Kelly, p. 166.

29. Kelly, p. 167.

30. Kelly, pp. 165-66.

31. Little, pp. 1319-20.

32. Little, p. 1320.

33. Mrs. D. W. Giles, introductory comments to the interview of Wesley Little, p. 1316.

34. Little, p. 1322.

35. Little, p. 1318.

36. Redmoun, p. 3265.

37. Redmoun, pp. 3266-68.

38. Heloise M. Foreman, introductory comments to the interview of Laura Redmoun, p. 3265.

39. Steven M. Tipton, *Getting Saved from the Sixties: Moral Meaning in Conversion and Cultural Change* (Berkeley: University of California Press, 1982), p. 282.

40. Kelly, p. 162.

41. Redmoun, p. 3267.

42. Potter, p. 24.

43. Kelly, pp. 165-167.

44. Redmoun, pp. 3266-67.

45. Mary Colbert, quoted in Rawick, vol. 12, p. 225.

46. Miss Catherine, quoted in Rawick, vol. 18, p. 214.

47. Jefferson Franklin Henry, quoted in Rawick, vol. 12, p. 192.

48. Stephen McCray, quoted in Rawick, vol. 7, p. 209.

49. Jack and Rosa Maddox, quoted in Rawick, Supplement 2, vol. 7, p. 2521.

50. Jack Maddox, pp. 2528-29.

51. Jack Maddox, pp. 2541-42.

5. SLAVE NARRATIVES, BLACK THEOLOGY OF LIBERATION, AND THE FUTURE

1. See James H. Cone, *Black Theology and Black Power* (New York: Seabury Press, 1969). In that text Cone defines black theology as the

explication of the meaning of the gospel from the perspective of the meaning of black oppressed people, who have experienced oppression by virtue of the fact that they were black (p. 117).

2. Gayraud Wilmore, "The New Context of Black Theology in the United States," in *Black Theology: A Documentary History, 1966-1979*, ed. Gayraud S. Wilmore and James H. Cone (Maryknoll, N.Y.: Orbis Books, 1979), p. 603.

3. Ibid. p. 605.

4. The term *thematic universe* is used here to refer to the religio-cultural universe that characterizes any historical experience and becomes the basis upon which people interpret their experience and struggles. Within this religio-cultural universe one receives clues to the values and sensibilities that determine the pre-textual awareness any community brings to its appreciation of the Christian texts. The notion of *thematic universe* is defined by Paulo Friere as constituting the "generative themes" within the world of the poor and refers to those symbols, images, concepts, and values that make up the pre-textual framework and grid through which the message of the gospel is seen.

5. Sallie McFague, *Speaking in Parables: A Study in Metaphor and Theology* (Philadelphia, Penn.: Fortress Press, 1975), pp. 3-4, 80-83, 175-78; idem, *Metaphorical Theology: Models of God in Religious Language* (Philadelphia, Penn.: Fortress Press, 1982), pp. 14-15, 103-44).

6. McFague, *Speaking in Parables*, p. 84.

7. Ibid. p. 3.

8. Ibid. pp. 66-87.

9. Gayraud S. Wilmore, "Black Theology: Review and Assessment," *Voices from the Third World*, vol. 5, no. 2 (1982), p. 14. For a further discussion of the debate among black theologians concerning this issue, see James H. Cone, "Epilogue: An Interpretation of the Debate Among Black Theologians," in Wilmore and Cone, *Black Theology*.

10. Rev. Bentley, quoted in Lawrence Levine, *Black Culture and Black Consciousness: Afro-American Folk Thought from Slavery to Freedom* (New York: Oxford University Press, 1981), p. 49.

11. Uncle Silas, quoted in Perdue, p. 100.

12. Choan-Seng Song, *Jesus, the Crucified People* (New York: Crossroad, 1990), pp. 102-3.

CONTRIBUTORS

Will Coleman is a doctoral candidate in philosophical and systematic theology at the Graduate Theological Union (Berkeley, California). His areas of research interests are theological hermeneutics, black theology, and African American Religious Thought.

George C. L. Cummings is a graduate of Union Theological Seminary (New York). Since 1987 he has been serving as associate professor of systematic theology at the American Baptist Seminary of the West and on the doctoral faculty of the Graduate Theological Union. He is author of the forthcoming *Black Theology USA and Latin American Liberation Theology*.

Dwight N. Hopkins has authored *Black Theology USA and South Africa: Politics, Culture, and Liberation* and edited, with Simon Maimela, *We Are One Voice: Essays on Black Theology in South Africa and the USA*. Currently working on *Shoes That Fit Our Feet: Sources for a Constructive Black Theology*, he teaches religious and ethnic studies at Santa Clara University (Santa Clara, California).

Cheryl J. Sanders is associate professor of Christian Ethics at Howard University School of Divinity. She received her Th.D. in applied ethics from Harvard Divinity School. Her dissertation is titled "Slavery and Conversion: An Analysis of Ex-slave Testimony." She is also associate pastor for leadership development at the Third Street Church of God in Washington, D.C.

INDEX